White Hat Leadership

White Hat Leadership

*How to Maximize Personal and
Employee Productivity*

T.R. Warren

Gibbs Smith, Publisher

TO ENRICH AND INSPIRE HUMANKIND

Salt Lake City │ Charleston │ Santa Fe │ Santa Barbara

First Edition
11 10 09 08 07   5 4 3 2 1

Published by
Gibbs Smith, Publisher
P.O. Box 667
Layton, Utah 84041

Orders: 1.800.835.4993
www.gibbs-smith.com

Designed by Michel Vrána, Black Eye Design
Printed and bound in the U.S.A.

Library of Congress Cataloging-in-Publication Data
Warren, T. R.
 White hat leadership : how to maximize personal and employee productivity /
T.R. Warren. — 1st ed.
    p. cm.
 ISBN-13: 978-1-4236-0109-8
 ISBN-10: 1-4236-0109-2
 1. Leadership. 2. Management. I. Title.

HD57.7.W376 2007
658.4'092—dc22

                                              2006032763

This book is dedicated to my mother, Jean Reeves Warren, a remarkable person who made all things possible. She gave me life, love, and lessons in perseverance. All that is good in me came from her and she remains the person I most admire in this world.

★ ★ ★

CONTENTS

★ ★ ★

★ ★ ★

ACKNOWLEDGMENTS

EVERY AUTHOR HAS HIS MUSES AND ENCOURAGERS AND I AM NO EXCEP-
TION. Without these people I would never have attempted to squeeze
writing a book into a business schedule that has me on the road two hundred days a year.

My family, already largely living without me, allowed me to retire to our
deck on nights and weekends to write. I am grateful for their generosity, for there
would be no book without their support.

Laurie Bullington was the first person to suggest that my thoughts are
worth putting onto paper. She less suggested than demanded it, so the very early
versions of this book were outlined years before there was an opportunity to pub-
lish. Even as I stumbled over content and complained about the process, Laurie
stayed the course, reading outlines, then editing drafts of chapters, and offering excellent insight to the value, or lack of value, of the content. There would
be no book without Laurie.

Dr. Linda Irby has long encouraged me to write. She kindly read an early
draft of this book, provided feedback, and pushed me forward with her positive
but candid critique.

Dr. Randy Harrington, my student and my mentor, is both brilliant and
inspiring, traits that forced me to "get game" when we became professional colleagues. Randy elevated my thought process, challenged my core beliefs about

myself, and thereby helped me trust my instincts to create my personal world-view. He is a friend of the highest order.

Fate handed me Gibbs Smith, my publisher, one cloudless afternoon in Sun Valley, Idaho, where he heard me speak to a group of bank executives. His first words to me were, "You should write a book, and I can help." Gibbs, I cannot thank you enough for your vote of confidence and for bringing your able team to this effort.

Lisa Anderson, my editor, came to me late in the process but immediately threw her heart and soul into the book. She is a wonderful collaborator and partner who kept me focused by bringing a long series of suggestions that improved the writing and organization. She's moved to other projects but I hope she returns for the second book.

There are many others, as there always are when books are published, and to all I offer this collective thank you.

★ ★ ★

LEADING CULTURES

I N THE MOVIES OF YESTERYEAR, before moral ambiguity and Clint Eastwood, we always knew the heroes and heroines; they wore the white hats. They had a code of conduct clearly evident to anyone who met them. They told the truth, took action, and led by example. Their integrity was unquestioned, their motives clear and pure, and their role unselfish. They sought not glory and instead worked to achieve the outcome best for all. They easily made friends, formed followers, and led the posse. The ultimate leaders, they also had the courage to go it alone if that's what it took to get the job done. We need those same heroes and heroines today.

Leading Cultures

MOST OF US BELIEVE LEADERS LEAD PEOPLE WHEN ACTUALLY LEADERS LEAD CULTURES. The CEO of a financial institution once described a failed mission. He observed, "We did everything right. We researched. We planned. We told people what we were going to do. We made assignments. Here I am a year later about to tell my board that we did not accomplish anything we set out to do. I don't know what we could have done differently, so this is frustrating and embarrassing."

It does appear the CEO did everything right, at least according to the business articles, books, and seminars. He had a great plan, a good system in place to implement the plan, and a staff of experienced people to make sure everything came together as designed. Yet his organization failed to accomplish its objectives. His statement implies that there was something wrong within the organization, but he did not know how or where to look for the answers. *White Hat Leadership* was written because of this confusion.

Every workplace has a culture.

IT IS IMPOSSIBLE FOR AN ORGANIZATION TO AVOID HAVING A CULTURE. Organizations create cultures involuntarily because people need to know the rules in order to function. In the absence of a strong leader who forces a defined culture upon the population, the population will create its own rules, which, collectively, become the culture. This is the greatest challenge for anyone desiring to provide a healthy, high-speed, highly productive work environment.

Culture consists of the sum of shared parts, including values, attitudes, behaviors, and language. Most importantly, it consists of shared values, hence a need to impose positive personal and corporate values upon the organization rather than to allow the culture to independently create its own value system. It is the culture that defines how we interact with each other and those who come into contact with the organization. Behavior is both a symptom and a result of culture, so how we deal with each other helps define a healthy versus a dysfunctional culture.

This means that the world created within an office or corporation evolves from every event that happens in the office or corporation, and every attitude, belief, and value expressed within it. The environment self-defines as we accept certain words, behaviors, attitudes, types of dialogue, groupings of people, and other elements that contribute to the culture stew.

Anthropologist Edward Hall defines three characteristics of culture: it is not innate but is learned; all facets of the culture are interrelated (meaning that if you affect a culture in one place, everything else is affected); and it is shared and effectively defines the boundaries of the group.[1]

Cultures can be defined, analyzed, built, dismantled, rebuilt, and controlled. Culture can also be positive or negative, helpful or hurtful, constructive or destructive. Culture cannot be eliminated.

CULTURES RULE ABOVE ALL OTHER INFLUENCES

GREAT PLANS AND SYSTEMS ARE OVERWHELMED BY ORGANIZATIONAL CULTURES THAT CREATE SIGNIFICANT BARRIERS TO SUCCESS. Harvard professor John P. Kotter, author of *Leading Change* and *A Force for Change* (among others), is a major researcher in this area and concludes that negative cultures can overwhelm even the best strategies created by an organization.[2] A list of writers as diverse as Jim Collins, Tom Peters, Daniel Goleman, and Jack Welch have concluded that other influences pale as a force when compared to the force of culture upon an organization. These giants of modern leadership theory have researched and delivered data that says we must understand and address our corporate culture in order to achieve corporate as well as personal potential.

Research has debunked the myth that there are always linear solutions to significant problems within work environments. Instead, we must look past systems into the way we function as a leadership team, management team, project team, and as an organization.

Being aware that culture exists means we can begin to examine the characteristics of culture and investigate possible intervention techniques. These characteristics give us the chance to demonstrate our White Hat leadership as we address problems that others fear to address, and offer solutions that others do not know exist.

CULTURES ARE PEOPLE BASED

ORGANIZATIONS ARE AND WILL REMAIN PEOPLE BASED, requiring an atmosphere of collaboration and creativity in order for the business to function at its fullest potential. Almost all the core principles offered here consider and respond to the motivators that remove negative aspects of culture while introducing positive responses to the needs of employees. The key to being a White Hat leader in a culture is pushing employees to the highest level of productivity while causing them to love it—and to know that you gave this environment to them.

Strategic planning is rarely people based, so strategy often is blunted or defeated because organizational cultures are not considered as a piece of the implementation process. This omission results in organizations that follow the normal rules of business to scratch their collective heads at their failure to achieve results.

Imprisoned by the concept of checklist leadership and model-motivated management, executives remain faced with the reality that great plans and great systems sometimes do not deliver great results. The problem in these cases is likely a dysfunctional culture that places barriers to trust, collaboration, commitment, and ultimately success. This is why organizations fail despite the fact they have expertise and experience, great plans and systems. Unfortunately, most CEOs (or leaders in any position) have yet to grasp this basic fact, choosing instead to return to strategic retreats where the same mistakes are repeated.

LEADERSHIP AND CULTURE

CULTURE IS CREATED AND THEREFORE CAN BE MANAGED AND CHANGED. The single greatest challenge of leadership is to overcome a negative culture and to maintain a positive culture.

Leading a culture has three parts: how we lead rather than what we lead; how well we work with each other versus how well we work; and how we succeed rather than whom we blame.

How we lead. White Hat leaders know who they are and what they can do to make a difference. As importantly, they communicate these factors to those around them, who become willing followers. This self-awareness of what is being seen and heard by others is part of the heroic process, for few can undertake the journey and fewer have the courage to stay the course.

Most people have some sense of the existence of the Divide, the gap between them and success. Beyond this "feeling," few can clearly identify the Divide and even fewer can articulate the barriers inherent to it. It is all but impossible to conquer the Divide when we are faced with its vagaries, but even more difficult when we know neither the specific problems offered up by the Divide or possible solutions to those problems. The search is for answers that define how we lead, the toolbox that does not contain all the answers but does contain concepts that can be used to fashion answers for specific situations.

Great leaders have a different vocabulary than the rest of us, a glossary of words, terms, and phrases that create a toolbox full of nifty metaphorical devices. This leadership vocabulary allows them to place leadership on a more intellectual plane toward the front of the brain, ever ready for recall on demand. Language is what allows each leader to think critically about a situation, process data (even intuitive data), and create a response that is built on knowledge, experience, and the tools at hand. Ironically, these tools are largely made up of what some call "soft skills" and others call "emotional quotient." Soft skills, the emotion-based analysis of other people, must ultimately reside within nature's most significant scientific tool (the human brain) as an intellectual resource in order to be fully utilized. Once housed inside the brain, soft skills are no longer soft; they are hard skills, applied in much the same way as numerical data. And therein lies the paradox. Soft skills are hard skills.

Culture analysis is sometimes considered "soft" leadership, but it is, in fact, the opposite. The quality of organizational culture actually enhances or hinders human productivity. Culture drives results in a way that strategy and process cannot. Yet organizational culture is so often ignored within organizations that it is no wonder that so many flounder when trying to define what is wrong. An organization that stays tuned to its culture is one that will succeed at the highest level, and a leader who knows how to correct a dysfunctional culture will stand out among his peers.

"Given our addiction to measurement," writes Marshall Goldsmith, founding director of the Alliance for Strategic Leadership, "you would think that we would be more attuned to measuring the 'soft side values' in the workplace: how often we're rude to people, how often we're polite, how often we ask for input rather than shut people out, how often we bite our tongue rather than spit out a needlessly inflammatory remark. Soft values are hard to quantify but, in the area of interpersonal performance, they are as vital as any number."[3]

> PERHAPS THERE WAS A TIME WHEN COMMAND AND CONTROL WAS THE RIGHT APPROACH . . . THAT TIME IS NO MORE.

The transition from numbers-driven, "bull in the china shop," command-style leadership to culture development style requires new tools of leadership. These tools are instantly usable and flexible enough to respond to most workplace situations.

How well we work with others versus how well we work. Command and control, the heavy-handed, top-down approach to management, has been the dominant leadership style in American organizations for the past four decades. Perhaps there was a time when command and control was the right approach: the time before technology ruled the workplace; the time before entrepreneurship inside and outside the organization replaced obedience; the time before employees asked "why"; the time when competition moved at a snail's pace, when the marketplace was stable, when people stayed with the same employer for forty years. That time is no more.

Today's technology has changed markets, created new internal and external pods for communicating information and spreading rumor, and made life and business move faster. Technology has sped innovation and rollouts of new products and services. It has created new employment opportunities that allow even a slightly annoyed employee to search for and find better opportunities.

Command-and-control leadership stifles innovation, frustrates good people who want to and can make a positive difference, and is too slow to adapt or to create and implement strategy with collaboration, staff support, and precision. In the top-down model, people do not act on behalf of the organization because they wait for permission. Morale is low and trust is lower. Everything flows downhill, one-way, creating corporate paralysis.

"We hurry and wait," said one VP of a financial institution. "Every step taken without direction is considered a misstep if not outright insubordination. No one offers a new idea. Why bother? Everything must originate from the top. That's how it works here. We are at a standstill."

In a business world that requires we be on the move, we stop. Corporations, even offices within corporations, are often perplexed as to why people will not seize the opportunity to problem solve, innovate, or, in the simplest terms, become self-driven. The answer is found in the culture of the operating group, regardless of its size. The answer is that people do not feel they are given permission to be engaged.

We know through a myriad of studies that self-managed teams accomplish more than single-leader teams. Environments that encourage independent thinking and action have higher levels of productivity. We know rules are necessary but we also know that rules created to cover the exception stifle the extraordinary.

The secret to achieving positive outcomes is a form of personal and corporate leadership I call "heroism" because it is based on leading with honesty and integrity, which moves people to work at the highest level of productivity and personal well-being. You can be a hero if you know how and then use what you know.

People who seek to lead organizations or consult to improve business culture are paying close attention to books and articles about the impact of interpersonal skills upon success, and the implication that successful leadership is based far more on our ability to form relationships than upon our ability to task. Key words continue to repeat themselves throughout the literature: collaboration, cooperation, integrity, truth, vulnerability, empathy, courage, values, and vision.

How we succeed instead of whom we blame. White Hat leaders always seek the outcome that serves the greater good. Conflict is welcome as long as it is issue-related rather than personal. Truth is preferred to creating an artificial sense of harmony that ignores the infamous "elephants in the room." Personal responsibility is a way of life, as is giving others credit for the work they perform, and success is shared. Reasons for decisions are revealed and integrity is honored. The blame game is replaced by a support system that mentors those who do make mistakes, without loss of accountability and consequences.

TRAITS OF A CULTURE

TRAITS THAT ARE COMMON TO CULTURES WILL, when understood, help heroes better implant positive values, attitudes, and behaviors upon a workplace.

An organization's culture can be examined in eight areas: interaction, association, satisfaction, self-protection, generalizations, fun, work tempo, and learning. These areas are interrelated and sometimes overlap. Yet each is a unique test of the ability of an organization to reach full potential while removing barriers to innovation and change.

The basis of these organizational assessments is taken from the anthropological work of Dr. Edward Hall. The assessment areas do not translate exactly into corporate culture, but adapting them is not hard.

Interaction. How we communicate with each other drives relationships, and relationships drive culture, which drives success. Interaction is defined as how we communicate with each other within and outside the organization. Dialogue is the core of culture. Although it is easy to narrowly define dialogue as conversation, it is equally a product of memoranda, e-mail, and intranet. Dialogue is any channel through which we exchange information and ideas.

E-mail, for example, is everywhere in today's business environment. It is a handy tool but can be inefficient for effective messaging. When people cannot see your face or hear your voice, you must choose your words carefully. Comments made in jest may be taken seriously; comments made in earnest may be interpreted as caustic; questions may be read as belittling, personal attacks.

Use punctuation in e-mail dialogue to help "translate" meaning. Let's look at a case of ineffective punctuation. A staff member forwarded an e-mail stating that he could not **DIALOGUE IS ANY CHANNEL THROUGH WHICH WE EXCHANGE INFORMATION AND IDEAS.** implement a project as assigned. He wrote that he would take another approach, which he described in detail. The supervisor's e-mail response was direct and clear, or so he thought: "Great. Thanks." This response was precisely what he meant to convey. "Great," meaning the new approach is accepted, and "thanks" for doing a good job.

The staff member did not perceive it this way. He believed the response was dripping with sarcasm, an interpretation that led him to write his own sarcastic and defensive e-mail. The venom of the message shocked the supervisor, so he sent an e-mail explaining his intentions. "I meant what I wrote," was his response.

The employee sent another nasty e-mail to the supervisor that was as defensive as the first. The supervisor reached for the telephone.

"Robert," he said, "that's enough. I wrote 'great' because your solution to the problem was great. I wrote 'thanks' because I am thankful for your creativity. Any sarcasm, cynicism, or criticism you read into those two works come from your imagination."

Robert protested that the e-mail was not written with affirmation, and that he was looking for affirmation. What did Robert need in the e-mail that he did not receive? Exclamation points! "Great! Thanks!" That additional punctuation demonstrates excitement and, to Robert, provides affirmation. E-mail has developed its own language.

Other forms of communication can indicate whether dialogue is positive or negative. Think of your meetings, for example. Meetings that start late, have hidden agendas, involve personal attacks (which can be as simple as rolling the eyes at a colleague's suggestion), ignore issues in order to avoid conflict, and forego accountability indicate the nature of dialogue is negative rather than positive. Rampant rumor mills and arguments in public places also indicate dysfunction.

These proverbial "elephants" in the organization are ignored, leading to employees' inability to effectively deal with each other. This becomes a detriment to maximizing the organization's success.

Leaders must have the courage to point to the elephants. But that's not enough. It is as important to state specifically what behavior you desire and what behavior you will not tolerate. This is a form of giving permission, as these "rules of engagement" define appropriate ways to communicate that will build healthy dialogue. You must address violators, preferably in private, in order to implant the behavior upon the organization. Should private redress not prove beneficial, then public redress at the moment of the violation will likely provoke a change. If not, you as a leader must take appropriate action to protect the culture.

This book gives much attention to dialogue within organizations. Pragmatic communication principles will be provided and explained so as to create a culture of positive interaction inside your office or organization.

Association. This trait has three elements. The first involves cliques, or the creation of exclusive subsets within the organization. These cliques consist of people with similar values, beliefs, and ambitions. By nature, members of cliques voluntarily restrict themselves to their group. The existence of cliques restricts relationships between other cliques and among people of different cliques. The goal is to create the opposite condition, inclusiveness, as inclusiveness promotes diverse collaboration.

White Hat leaders must convert cliques into pods. Pods require members of cliques to roam across the organization rather than being confined to a single subset of people.

A pod has to be created by artificial means; it does not naturally evolve like cliques do. Projects and task forces are excellent means for creating pods. The key is to diversify the membership of the pod, just as you should diversify the entire workforce. This opens possibilities for creativity and collaboration, both of which enhance productivity. For example, an IT project that delivers service to the front lines will usually be directed by an executive and a team from IT. But including someone from customer service (a frontline employee) who provides input from the ultimate user, as well as someone from marketing who may perceive an outreach opportunity, would improve both the service and the organization's culture through cross departmental collaboration. This integrates various areas of the organization, breaking down cliques, which improves the culture while adding the benefit of perspectives outside the linear aspects of the project.

The second part of association is the philosophy of superiority, or the belief of an employee that he or she is intrinsically superior to the others and is therefore an alpha figure. This condition is also known as "the pecking order," a phrase Dr. Hall claims evolved from the act of chickens determining which chicken may peck another, resulting in a structured hierarchy among a group of chickens confined to a pen.[4]

Certain employees often foster pecking orders if they can be at or near the top, satisfying their need for attention and influence while creating the appearance of status. Pecking orders make collaboration impossible to achieve because a hierarchy exists that overpowers any meaningful exchange of ideas. After all, if one person is ranked lower than another, then his ability to persuade the person above him is small. Even if someone on the low end of the pecking order may be allowed input, the existence of the pecking order signals that it may be inappropriate to do so. People use the pecking order to symbolize superiority of one over another, reduce dissent within the discussion, and aid in implementing personal agendas.

Segments of the book will offer ways to counter cliques and pecking orders through communication and leadership techniques. For example, returning to the IT service project example, the IT executive is the likely choice to lead because IT will create the process. The lowest-paid person inside the pod—the person lowest on the pecking order—represents the service aspect of the project and the end user. This person will probably act reserved unless thrust into a leadership role, such as chairing the project. This simple appointment destroys the pecking order that is implied by position and salary. Most leaders would not put such a person in charge, out of concern that she is in over her head, for she is a frontline employee with little knowledge of technology. However, we must keep in mind that the final user is the service provider so this is a *service* product delivered through IT rather than being an IT project. The end user is in the best position to know if the project delivers what is needed on the front lines, so her ascent to head the committee is not unreasonable. The expertise from IT is still there in the person of the IT executive. Changing the pecking order helps, even demands, a healthy layer of input from the end use. In addition, the changing of the pecking order is healthy within the organization because it recognizes the value of other areas of the organization which will foster ideas in the future.

The third element is called positive association and it is a barrier buster. This association embodies shared corporate values that complement the employees' values, with a focus on a common mission/vision. Interaction occurs across departments, expertise, and projects, and most importantly, it slashes through organizational charts as if the boxes on the charts do not exist. Fluidity throughout the organization allows good ideas to spread with speed, encouraging quick examination of the idea and faster execution of the development and implementation stages. In simple terms, positive association means the cliques are removed and people are working with each other inside clear values and toward a common goal. Competition between individuals and among groups, evidenced by pecking orders, is replaced by collaboration and cooperation to reach goals that have been clearly articulated. Dialogue is open and expressive because the emphasis is on truth rather than on harmony, and there is an absence of blame. Positive association means that business is not personal and that success is a group effort. As a result, self-interest is subordinated in favor of what is best for the whole organization.

Future chapters will discuss how heroes can emphasize core corporate values so that all employees know the parameters of acceptable behavior. Open dialogue should be encouraged and blame games not tolerated. Relationship and trust-building skills should be taught through formal education and corporate retreats. Everyone in the corporation should be aware of the value that each department brings to the organization, and their successes should be celebrated as a success for all. This may require a new internal communication model that shares information across all departments. Cross-departmental committees, visioning groups, and task forces should be normal ways of conducting business.

Satisfaction. Employee satisfaction comes from knowing what is expected from them, employees having the ways and means to meet expectations, and being provided the opportunity to demonstrate their abilities.

Corporate America tends to be driven by the philosophy that money and position create satisfaction for employees. This is not wholly true, although all of us will accept the money. In Adrian Gostick and Chester Elton's book on recognition programs, *Managing with Carrots*, the authors cite a study that indicates good pay and benefits do not rank in the top ten items that create a satisfying workplace.[5]

People who lean toward cooperation, relationships, and achieving and sharing success as a group or organization will find satisfaction working with a team. These people will work on behalf of the organization with limited self-interest because they operate with a sense of humility.

On the opposite side are negative satisfaction points that include pushing a personal agenda, advancing personal success at the expense of others, and a focus on glory for a unit rather than for the organization as a whole. The presence of these tendencies demonstrates the importance of emphasizing core values, including humility and integrity, over self-interest.

Some companies perform exit interviews as an employee departs to ask why the employee is leaving. The answers are predictable: a raise, a better position, or the new job is closer to home. The real question to ask is "Why were you *looking* for a job?" This moves the organization closer to the truth while revealing where and how the organization has failed to provide job satisfaction for the employee. The value of asking this question to departing employees is that the collection of data becomes research that exposes consistent failings within the culture. The articulation of these failings provides leaders ample justification for creating positive change.

Recognizing the impact of employee satisfaction on turnover, productivity, and positive interaction, future chapters will identify the importance of expressing employee value, understanding and leveraging employee "cravings," and using communication styles that increase loyalty.

Self-protection. Self-protection results from the absence of trust, which is manifested in the lack of perceived goodwill among colleagues. Absence of trust limits dialogue and destroys effective collaboration as individuals seek to protect themselves from criticism and blame.

Self-protection is a product of the command-and-control leadership act of killing the messenger of bad news. If messengers are shot, no one will be willing to deliver bad news or new ideas. Rejection of truth leads to subterranean hostility. Rejection of ideas leads to paralysis of creative problem solving.

Organizations in which most individuals protect themselves are highly politicized. You can detect this behavior in meetings by observing those who are defensive, center on individual goals, cover their butts, and "suck up" rather than focus on teamwork and maximum performance for the organization. These individuals play the blame game with viciousness.

Acts of self-protection have a powerfully negative impact on positive association. They lead to low morale, which may translate into higher turnover rates.

The only way to rid an organization of this bunker mentality is to create rules of courteous behavior, avoid personal attacks by keeping conversation centered on issues, and by having consequences for individuals who engage in ridicule and blame.

REJECTION OF TRUTH LEADS TO SUBTERRANEAN HOSTILITY. REJECTION OF IDEAS LEADS TO PARALYSIS OF CREATIVE PROBLEM SOLVING.

The culture change is driven by clearly articulated value systems operating simultaneously with immediate negative feedback to unacceptable behavior. Both actions are addressed in the pages ahead.

Generalizations. People who tend to categorize individuals by thinking in general terms about an entire segment of the population have difficulty dealing with people, promoting positive associations, and making healthy decisions on behalf of the organization.

These generalizations often involve race or gender bias, but can also involve bias about age, length of service (seniority), political leanings, and sexual preference. A person who generalizes creates tremendous barriers to achieving a healthy and productive organization. Instead, the person alienates or deliberately isolates personnel from dialogue and projects, not to mention bringing about possible legal ramifications.

Blatant bias is intolerable, harmful, and may even be illegal, but subtle bias can just as effectively limit opportunities for an individual or group. Generalizations create a high degree of hostility in the workplace, foster mistrust, and thwart collaboration. A company that has a high degree of generalization among its employees is always a company that has no identifiable value system, leaving it to others to fill this void with their own negative value system. Dialogue in such settings often uses violent language to express unrest, such as: "The next time she does that to me I'm going to slap her." "If I had a gun I'd shoot him." "Sometimes I wish I could blow up this place." Other signs are use of derisive language about a colleague, such as, "This guy's just an idiot." Anger management is often an issue within this culture so there is often a strong sense of tension among some employees.

People in management positions who demonstrate generalization need additional counseling and training; otherwise, their attitudes and personnel decisions that stem from those attitudes will foster a negative culture. Few organizations move decisively against this behavior. This delay in action is often an anxiety-avoidance response, meaning the stress of dealing with the condition is so great that we avoid confronting it. Courage, anxiety, and overcoming barriers to change are fully discussed within.

Fun. This is a major but often ignored element of a healthy culture. The power of fun means people are able to enjoy each other and the work they perform.

Many studies indicate that fun and innovation go hand in hand, as do fun and motivation. It certainly makes sense that the ability to share humor with colleagues opens doors to inclusiveness and collaboration, both attributes of a healthy organization.

A Yale School of Management study on the effect of mood on productivity concluded that laughter is the fastest mood virus in a business venue. Laughter lifts spirits, which increases cooperation and productivity. The act of laughing, concludes the Yale study, actually improves the brain's ability to perform work.[6]

Permission giving is important to leadership. Fun often requires permission as people may worry that superiors who are all about work frown upon laughter in the office. Discouraging fun at work is a control-management tool left over from ancient days. Leaders must give permission to employees to elevate the elements of positive culture.

Likewise, leaders must withdraw permission for attitudes and behaviors that create a negative culture. The absence of fun fine tunes a culture that fosters anxiety, depression, and dislike of someone with whom or for whom you work partially by reducing the mental capabilities associated with productivity. The nature of "fun" is also an indicator of whether a culture is healthy or ill. An organization that is all work and no play may possess a strong negative undercurrent that is sometimes exposed by "sick," dark, cynical humor.

Work tempo. Work tempo and attention to time indicates an appreciation for the needs of colleagues and the organization. It is defined by how quickly the organization reaches its desired output. Is the tempo upbeat, even urgent? If so, this shows that the people within the organization want to serve their company and colleagues by being responsive. Employees will answer e-mails within twenty-four hours. People will arrive to meetings on time, and they will be prepared to openly discuss issues. Employees search for ways to work together, share ideas, and help each other.

Observe how long it takes to receive a return phone call or get a response to an e-mail, how many people are late for a meeting, and how often employees miss deadlines. Great cultures are sensitive to time and the tempo of the work.

A low work tempo is often exposed by a slow response rate to requests for information. Habitual tardiness to meetings is another sign of slow tempo. A high number of canceled meetings and forgotten prearranged phone conversations indicate employees are more concerned with their work than the overall success of the organization. An absence of buy-in to vision and projects is often the cause of these failures to respond.

Leaders must implant a sense of urgency upon employees in order to achieve maximum results. Lacking this urgency, the organization may foster procrastination and lose the productivity of those who depend upon the procrastinator. High-tempo organizations have high-context messages that avoid confusion and delay. Positive association must exist to facilitate collaboration and cooperation on projects. Issues are in the open to be discussed and dialogue is cordial and open to criticism and suggestions. Trust levels are very high. Creating these culture points are covered in detail in this book.

Learning. Learning is another hallmark of a healthy organization. The capacity of each individual to respond to change directly relates to that individual's willingness to learn. A great leader is eager to identify the willingness to learn, the ability to learn, and the best ways to learn within each unit and for each individual. A leader uses formal education and self-education to better himself and encourages others to do the same. All great cultures place significant emphasis on constantly improving the knowledge and communication skills of employees.

One of the major themes of this book is the necessity to continue learning as part of preparing to be an effective leader. In addition, continuation of study (formal or informal) will also encourage reading of books and magazines by staff. Offer use of corporate computers before work, during lunch, and after hours so employees can take online courses from a community college or university. This costs the organization nothing while providing a relevant service to your workforce.

> THE CAPACITY OF EACH INDIVIDUAL TO RESPOND TO CHANGE DIRECTLY RELATES TO THAT INDIVIDUAL'S WILLINGNESS TO LEARN.

In addition, certificate-granting courses or degree-granting courses give the organization a more knowledgeable employee, which is a benefit to the company. Younger employees are most likely to use this benefit.

Also, send up-and-coming employees to seminars and conferences that prepare them for what comes next in their careers versus what they presently do. This not only prepares them for advancement but also reveals to them the reasons why their managers conduct business as they do. This added connection between employee and supervisor creates a better dynamic for the organization.

Leaders cannot afford to ignore the debilitating effects of a negative culture.

Those working in a negative culture fail to reach full personal and professional potential, costing the organization productivity and profits while contributing to the employee's unhappiness with the job.

On the employee level, this is connected to a feeling of losing control. Control in this sense does not mean power, but rather means a loss of personal value, the absence of affirmation from others, and the pain of watching those promoting self-interest achieve recognition from the organization. This powerlessness leads to underground aggression.

The absence of reaching potential, especially when the organization clearly does not offer alternative avenues to growth, creates a series of recognizable phases that evolve into a destructive employee. The employee first feels emptiness, a longing for what is missing, before entering a stage of frustration that finally leads to anger manifested in overt or covert aggressive behavior.

Once unhappy, these employees are only happy when everyone else is unhappy. To deal with these feelings an employee begins to rationalize that the company owes something to the employee, something that helps pay for the pain inflicted. This may manifest itself in simple ways at first, such as stealing supplies from the stockroom. Over time, this progresses to lying on expense accounts, taking computers or televisions, and other forms of theft.

The anger also demonstrates itself in other types of negative behavior. The individual may stymie reports, alienate vendors and customers, backstab fellow employees, spread false rumors that hurt the company, and in ways great and small make it difficult for others to perform their jobs and be happy employees.

Keep in mind that this agitated state exists because the organization does not leverage its resources to advance the abilities and well-being of its employees. Instead, it chooses to advance only the few on a selected basis according to what may be described as negative criteria. Bad managers are promoted to corner offices. Good executive assistants remain in their cubicles.

This is an important lesson about culture. Leaders and managers cannot afford to ignore the debilitating effects that a negative culture can have on human beings. Yet, culture as a barrier or facilitator to success is almost always ignored. Instead, we look for shallow answers to questions that are much more complex than we wish to admit. For all these reasons and more, leaders must directly address elements of dysfunctional culture and the people attached to them.

POSITIVELY IMPACT YOUR CULTURE AND MAKE IT BETTER.

It is the responsibility of a heroic leader to conduct an audit of the organization's culture and then to address its issues.

Good leaders observe. Employee actions tell us a great deal about the state of our organizational culture. In addition, good leaders listen *and* hear. There is a difference between the two words. One may listen to what is being said without ever hearing the message, the real content and the meaning of what is said.

For example, we have all attended meetings that were designed to gain buy-in from all participants to some project. We have heard people say, "I am good to go with this." Yet, the project stumbles, stalls, and then fails.

"I'm good to go with this" may in fact mean, "I'll not get too involved because (1) I do not really understand this assignment, (2) I do not want to be a party to a possible failure, (3) I do not care, or (4) all of the above."

The culture of your organization is shaped and exhibited by the way people think, problem solve, engage in dialogue, respond to accountability, and lead and follow. Culture is also shaped and exhibited by titles, office space, furniture, views from the window, parking spots, reward and recognition systems, and a myriad of small things.

The good news is that you can positively impact your culture and make it better. This requires (1) self-awareness, (2) people awareness, and (3) communication awareness. The following chapters will guide you in successfully building a positive culture.

The section on self-awareness acknowledges that White Hat leaders must define who they are and, perhaps key to the process, to decide who they want to be. The distance between these two, called the Divide, must be closed during the journey to hero status. Self-awareness also requires that we follow a bit of wisdom from Albert Einstein: The person who leads must first lead himself.

People awareness, along with other chapters, teaches how a heroic leader steps away from his people to assess what really drives them to excellence, and then goes about the task of providing those drivers.

Communication awareness offers pragmatic communication modeling on two levels. The first is how to communicate within a culture, while the second level teaches communication tips that will save time, motivate employees, and increase productivity.

This book is not simply about leadership. This book is about becoming a hero.

★ ★ ★

CHAPTER ONE

★ ★ ★

CHANGE THE WAY YOU THINK ABOUT LEADERSHIP

White Hat Principles:

- ★ *Leadership is your vocation.*
- ★ *Leadership is often about knowing when and how to lean on intuition versus data.*
- ★ *Leadership is about standing for something.*
- ★ *The best leaders connect who they are with what they do.*
- ★ *Leadership is about relationships.*

BEFORE LEARNING TO LEAD OTHERS, we first must learn to lead ourselves. This begins with an understanding of who we are. The best leaders understand themselves, but most of us do not, except on the most superficial level. We all have an intuitive understanding, of course, but most of us would have to fake a realistic evaluation of who we are. I once asked a class of senior management executives to perform the simple task of writing their five highly personal core values that drive the way they deal with their family and business colleagues. I watched their eyes rise to the ceiling as they began to contemplate the assignment. At that point I delivered the final instruction: you have twenty seconds. This created much anxiety among the class; in fact, more than ninety percent could not fulfill the assignment in twenty seconds because, in reality, they had no idea what the answer was. One person wrote five personal values in twelve seconds, meaning not only did she have superb writing skills, but also an advantage. "I did this exercise when I started my journal for self-improvement," she reported. "At first, these were the values I wanted to communicate to those around me but had not embraced to the point that I could consistently deliver them. Now they truly are my values." This was the third day of a leadership session that had divided the group into four teams. This woman had been selected by her colleagues as their team captain. "That's one reason I voted for her," remarked a teammate. "I had this sense that she was very self-contained and that gave me confidence in her ability to lead us." This observation removed the need for the thirty-minute lecture I had planned because it demonstrated how clearly articulated values allow others to understand and trust us at a level that motivates them to follow us with confidence.

THE TRUTH IS THAT MANY PEOPLE ASPIRE TO BE LEADERS BUT FEW WILL PREPARE. THOSE WHO BECOME EFFECTIVE LEADERS ARE THE ONES WHO PREPARE TO LEAD.

One of the "aha" moments for her and her colleagues was realizing that we usually write values representing who we *want* to be rather than who we are. We grow into the value system by making a conscious attempt to live them. Eventually, living within the value system becomes second nature. Over time, these do become our values and our conduct reflects this growth.

Attaining this state of self-awareness requires a measure of soul searching that demands honesty about the person you are as well as the leader you want to be. The truth is that many people aspire to be leaders but few will prepare. Those who become effective leaders are the ones who prepare to lead.

The process of preparation is most difficult at the beginning because we are, as noted above, most likely *redefining* ourselves. Indeed, our initial examination tends to be negative. Typical self-observations become a menu of negative traits we know we possess but that we have not been dedicated to changing. This list may include observations about our behavior such as the following:

* ★ *Readiness to criticize others*
* ★ *A tendency to dismiss criticism of ourselves*
* ★ *Making decisions without input from those affected by the decisions*
* ★ *Impatience with staff*
* ★ *A tendency to punish people who make mistakes*
* ★ *A temper that makes us say things that hurt others*

* *Poor team-building skills*
* *An aversion to making difficult decisions quickly*
* *Fear of delegation*
* *Poor interpersonal skills and mentoring skills*
* *Poor conflict resolution skills*

This list can become long when people honestly consider their past conduct. A more positive approach is to begin by outlining the traits of leaders who have instilled respect and loyalty in us. This outline provides a comparison between what we observe as traits of effective leaders and how *we* interact with corporate goals and staff. Modeling our behavior on the behavior of people we know to be effective is a great way to identify our own strengths and weaknesses. This still requires a list of areas where we must improve, but it does so in the context of what we hope to achieve.

Learning to lead oneself is not a mental game. The self-analysis should be written so that it stays at the forefront of our everyday thoughts and deeds. In

WHEN WE SET A GOOD EXAMPLE THROUGH VALUES, WE ILLUSTRATE THE BEHAVIOR WE EXPECT FROM OTHERS AS THEY INTERACT WITH EACH OTHER AND CONDUCT THEIR BUSINESS.

addition, the simple process of writing increases the psychological commitment to complete this exercise, which will take an extended period of time to be fully implemented. The two rules of success are review and update. Patience and persistence are the values you must employ in order to attain the desired result.

The White Hat principles in this chapter emphasize the need for each of us to conduct an internal analysis of our level of commitment. Doing so results in our ability to lead by example, and thereby demonstrate to others how we interact with people and how we conduct business. In addition, when we set a good example through values, we illustrate the behavior we expect from others as they interact with each other and conduct their business. Just as important, we establish ourselves as people worthy of leadership positions, as well as people who deserve the loyalty of the staff.

Use the five principles to reposition your traditional views about what leadership means and what comprises an effective leader. The first principle abandons the traditional view that your vocation is your job and that leadership is situational. Instead, leadership is your vocation, an "every day and in every way" approach to your working life. The second principle rejects the concept that leadership should emphasize knowledge of tasks (yours and everybody else's). It is more important to understand the nuances of the work environment. The third principle recognizes that great leaders define themselves in such strong terms that the rest of us know their core values. The fourth principle establishes that we all operate at a higher level when we personally connect to the work. The fifth principle sums the wisdom of the first three: leadership is predominantly about how we establish and use relationships. This concluding principle flies headlong into the philosophy of command-and-control management—by motivating employees through communication, good leaders achieve loyalty, whereas command-and-control leadership simply achieves compliance.

Consider each principle and what it means in redefining the word *leadership*. In doing so, you will open your mind to eliminating negative corporate cultures and increasing human productivity—that of your followers, your leaders, and yourself.

GOOD LEADERS RECOGNIZE THAT LEADERSHIP SHOULD BE THE GOAL OF EVERY EMPLOYEE, MANAGER, AND EXECUTIVE, BECAUSE LEADING INVOLVES CONTRIBUTING TO THE COMPANY'S VISION AND WELFARE.

This pragmatic, holistic approach to leadership intertwines multiple elements into our understanding of what leadership means and how it presents itself to us and others. Although leadership must contain some practical everyday skills, especially in the way we view our followers and communicate to them, there are times when leaders must be attuned to an ambiguous culture in order to be responsive.

This is a journey for all, not only the few who are working from leadership positions. Good leaders recognize that leadership should be the goal of every employee, manager, and executive, because leading involves contributing to the company's vision and welfare. They believe that leadership must arise from anywhere in the organization because great corporate vision is a collaborative effort that seeks input, from the executive suite to the vendor at the delivery door.

Leadership is your vocation.

YOUR WORK IS NOT YOUR VOCATION. Your vocation is "leader." Secretary or CEO, you must seek out ways to make a positive difference whether the area you influence is as small as a workroom or as large as a company.

Most of America's Worker Bees (WBs) feel defined by their offices or cubicles.

They restrict their corporate involvement to the duties in the job description. Their command-and-control supervisors may like the fact that the WBs are contained in a tightly defined space. This keeps them under control and clueless to the vision, values, and workings of the organization. Unable to ask questions and make suggestions, the WBs become the proverbial cogs in the corporate engine, compliant but not committed.

A call to lead is a call to *do more*. That invitation creates fear in the hearts of those who find security inside the cubicle. This fear causes them to give up their power to make a difference, leaving the vision, values, and decisions of the company in the hands of others.

There is a significant downside to this attitude for both employee and organization. The "forfeit from fear syndrome" results in the Worker Bee's sacrificing his or her ability to have some control over the type of work and quality of life he or she will experience at the company.

There is also a loss on the corporate side because supervisors who allow WBs to exist sacrifice the intellect and energy WBs can bring to an organization. Good leaders, wherever they are inside the company, have a higher calling. They recognize that office walls cannot restrict them or their staff unless they allow it. Offices are where we do what we do for a living, but they certainly do not define who we are. Whether a vice president, secretary, accountant, personnel manager, marketer, or scientist, each of us has the ability to contribute to the company's welfare and to our own personal happiness.

Understood in this way, leadership becomes a community-wide function, available to all who dare to take the plunge. Everyone should commit to being a leader; in so doing, we gain greater input into our work and personal lives. Everyone in a leadership position must give others permission to assume leadership roles, expanding the view and influence of employees so that their input at all levels is encouraged and rewarded.

Leadership is often about knowing when and how to lean on intuition versus data.

LEADERSHIP IS OFTEN ABOUT FEEL AND THE CONFIDENCE TO KNOW WHEN TO LEAN ON INTUITION VERSUS DATA. Like improvisation, it is the ability to act in an unbalanced moment. We need something more than the mechanics to be a winner—we must be able to read the intrinsic signs of our organizational culture in order to seize an opportunity to be the winner.

The flaw of "leadership formation" classes is that they are about mechanics, or tasking. For example, one leadership seminar spends a day on the subject of financial ratios. Although this subject may be important, it is disingenuous to place it within a leadership seminar as it more appropriately belongs in a management or financial seminar. A segment on how to process a loan application also addresses a task function. This rote learning, no better than memorizing the periodic table in chemistry or the words of the Gettysburg Address, spoon-feeds facts and models without teaching people how to think, where to place data so it has the correct context, and how to use the information provided.

"Data dialing" is a term describing the phenomenon of people seeking answers in numbers, trends, and patterns to the exclusion of experience, observation, and anecdotal evidence, the total of which creates intuition. When they need answers, these people simply dial up the data and go where the numbers lead them. This reliance on numbers means that database leadership has no adaptability or fluidity.

NUMBERS MIGHT BE INDICATORS OR PREDICTORS, BUT SHOULD NEVER BE CONSIDERED AS ABSOLUTELY DEFINITIVE.

Good leadership emphasizes the second half of the word "leadership"—the word "ship." Captaining a ship requires nautical knowledge, for certain. It also takes feel and the confidence to make decisions in the moment based upon several factors. A great captain constantly checks the current, wind, and weather, and keeps fine-tuning the abilities of the crew.

This point of view was proven when I became a crew member during a regatta in San Diego Bay. We had an exceptional captain who trained the neophytes (which included me) on the basics of sailing, and called out our moves as the race commenced. We followed orders—and we won. Between races, I asked how the captain knew precisely when to make those moves. He said, "In the end, it is about feel. All the other captains know the same mechanics I do. The difference in winning and not winning is not about the mechanics. You have to feel the boat and sense your people. We'll do even better the second time," he added, "because I've watched you move, seen the speed at which you execute commands, and I have a sense of the winds. Yeah, I can really feel it now." Indeed, we won again by a larger margin.

All the rival captains possessed equal nautical skills, but my captain was able to sense and synthesize the variables of water, wind, and crew and combine them for a winning result.

My present experience with executives in leadership positions is that they tend to perform more data dialing than is healthy. As one CEO put it, "You can always blame the numbers." Blame the numbers? People are behind the numbers. Look past the numbers and pay attention to the needs of people and the culture created by the leadership style and abilities of those participating at all levels. Numbers might be indicators or predictors, but should never be considered as absolutely definitive.

The point is that a lesser personnel (and personal) performance inevitably results when we place too much emphasis on the mechanical/tasking side of the equation. The ultimate goal is always to optimize individual performance, which, in turn, optimizes corporate performance.

Seminar gurus want us to believe there is some great core truth to the task education model. So let me ask you two blunt questions: How many hours have you sat through these stand-up routines? Out of the total hours spent on your butt listening intently and taking copious notes, how many of those hours contained one iota of information that you used when you returned to your job?

A LESSER PERSONNEL (AND PERSONAL) PERFORMANCE INEVITABLY RESULTS WHEN WE PLACE TOO MUCH EMPHASIS ON THE MECHANICAL/TASKING SIDE OF THE EQUATION.

The answer is maybe one percent, if you are really dedicated to using what you hear. The gurus tell you what, but not how and rarely why. They assure you something works, but you find out that it doesn't work when you get back to the organization. And the facts and models have not produced a better leader. Maybe they produced a better manager, which is the best result we can gain from these programs.

These are only methods. Methods change. Principles never change.

Clay Christensen, who developed the idea of disruptive innovation, concludes, "The whole enterprise of teaching managers is steeped in the ethic of data-driven statistical support. The problem is that data is only available about the past. So the way we've taught managers to make decisions and consultants to analyze problems condemns them to take action when it is too late."[1]

What is missing is building the instinctive, core leadership abilities that are buried within us, sometimes deep inside. Discovering these elements and using pragmatic principles will not happen until you commit to becoming a leader. The rest of this book will help you uncover the elements of intuition.

Leadership is about standing for something.

LEADERS SHOULD MAKE EVERY EFFORT TO DESCRIBE THEMSELVES IN TERMS THAT PREPARE THE TROOPS FOR FUTURE DECISIONS AND ACTIONS. The world of psychology has a theory called "the tendency to self-define." The theory holds that we should clearly define ourselves to others, for if we do not, people will define us as they please. Most of the time, proposes the theory, people will define us negatively.

WE SHOULD CLEARLY DEFINE OURSELVES TO OTHERS, FOR IF WE DO NOT, PEOPLE WILL DEFINE US AS THEY PLEASE.

Recall the 2001 story of Chandra Levy, the aide to Congressman Gary Condit. After it became known that the woman had been murdered, the congressman decided to withhold any comment. Further investigation revealed that the congressman and the aide had engaged in a sexual affair. Congressman Condit remained silent.

The investigation of the murder became national news, fostering columns and television panel discussions about the murder and the congressman's role as a possible suspect. In the void of Condit's own words, the pundits as well as the public had plenty of room to speculate, and speculate they did. Condit was convicted of murder in the forum of public opinion, although he was later officially cleared. His mistake, other than his own misconduct with the aide, was that he left a void that other people were eager to fill with their scenarios.

The theory of self-defining had played itself in full public view. With only the scant evidence available, and no clear definition of the congressman as anything other than that offered in public discourse, he was defined in the most negative of terms. This scenario plays out on the smaller stage of offices and companies, communities, and families.

"Who are you, really?" my oldest son inquired of me one day. Obviously I had done a poor job of defining myself, and now my twenty-three-year-old son wanted an answer. The answer took a lot of thought and several typed pages. It was the most important document I ever wrote because it answered legitimate questions about my beliefs and why I conduct myself as I do. It was important for me to define myself to help my son see his father in full light.

Employees don't ask these questions outright, but they want to know the answers. The more they know you—the real you—the better they understand and accept you.

Consider the following business case study. A VP of a company wants her people to feel free to complain about her division's decisions for a number of reasons. She believes morale will be higher when employees feel free to voice their opinions. She also believes that the division will benefit from the solutions that will, hopefully, result from responding to the complaints. She also understands that open complaining may prevent the vitriolic culture that often evolves when complaints are driven underground. She believes this open access policy will provide her an opportunity to specifically address the issues upsetting her staff.

Her invitation is met with silence.

The VP later discovers that no one believes she is sincere. In fact, employees view the request as a corporate witch-hunt for troublemakers. Finding themselves under what they view as an attempt to stifle their concerns, they take complaining further underground while adding a layer of paranoia.

LOOK PAST THE NUMBERS AND PAY ATTENTION TO THE NEEDS OF PEOPLE AND THE CULTURE CREATED BY THE LEADERSHIP STYLE AND ABILITIES OF THOSE PARTICIPATING AT ALL LEVELS.

The VP's shortcoming is that she had too long avoided defining herself as an open-door person who embraced discussion with her employees, so this sudden redefinition of her value system was hard for them to accept. In other words, she had become a victim of the theory of self-definition. Without a definition, the staff had defined her in a negative way, and attitudes, like concrete, harden over time. Her attempts to define herself came too late for this effort to be a success, so she became a victim of her past sins.

The danger of negative definition is most important at two points in a leader's career. The first is when leadership is new, carrying with it no baggage but also no image. The second occurs when an established leader begins to act in a way that contradicts his or her history of behavior.

A new leader must explain his value and belief system as soon as possible; otherwise, the employees are likely to filter all future decisions through their self-definition of the leader. New leaders should make every effort to describe themselves in terms that prepare the staff for future decisions and actions, such as revealing core value systems and modeling behavior early on.

When a leader is well established in a company, she faces the dangers of defining herself too late because the employees have a filter system in place. The VP described above found herself in this situation. Her call to employees to share concerns was not consistent with previous behavior, thereby resulting in the employees' suspicion that she had a negative motive for this new behavior. She should have been sensitive enough to know this so she could address her staff. This could have been easily accomplished by a simple mea culpa.

"I know in the past that I have not been receptive to your criticisms," she could have said. "I have come to the realization that this attitude is bad for you, bad for me, and bad for the company. That's changing now. Please bring your concerns to me, and your solutions as well. This is important to me and I would appreciate your help. I promise that I will accept that your comments intend to help all of us and that every concern, even those that may make me personally uncomfortable, will be welcome. I will not think less of you. In fact, I will treasure you even more. Please, share your concerns with me."

> THE PERSON WHO IS HAPPIEST HAS FORMULATED A CLEAR PICTURE OF WHO SHE IS AND WHAT SHE REPRESENTS. SHE WORKS FOR AN ORGANIZATION THAT AGREES WITH HER PERSONAL VALUE SYSTEM.

This statement defines the value beyond corporate outcomes and redefines the VP in positive terms. She also honestly and humbly addresses her previous behavior so that the staff can begin its own process of rehabilitating her image. Most importantly, the VP defines herself.

It is difficult to rehabilitate an image, so the best course of action is to avoid the possibility of negative definition. However, we can rehabilitate our images by admitting to less desirable actions of the past while consistently reinforcing the new image over time.

Many years ago an academic study revealed why some employees are happy and some are not happy.

The end results are not surprising. The person who is happiest has formulated a clear picture of who she is and what she represents. She works for an organization that agrees with her personal value system, even if only on an intuitive level. The organization values her as an employee and she values her place within the organization. Finally, she views herself as one person in an organization of many people that, collectively, makes a positive difference in the community. This means her value is multiplied by the value of others, thereby creating even greater value for herself.

One of your goals as leader is to create this work environment for those who report to you.

The best leaders connect who they are with what they do.

ACTING UPON THOSE THINGS THAT FIT YOUR CORE BEING MAKES LEADERSHIP NATURAL. This is why the ambition to be a CEO rarely translates to happiness once the person achieves the goal. The title or role doesn't generate satisfaction and productivity; rather, connecting to our own personal values and interests drives our satisfaction and productivity. Great leadership most effectively evolves when we sail the ship we love.

This is a profound connection. We all know people in leadership positions who are not leaders. You may also know people in your organization who lead from positions not ordinarily defined as leadership positions. Engagement in their lives pushes this "need to lead." These people, with rare exception, love what they do because it connects to their self-identity.

A friend of mine recounts a story of being vice president of information services for a financial institution. For a decade he toiled in that role as, in his words, "a reactor."

"I was told to do this and do that," he says. "Make this thing happen to help marketing and make that thing happen to improve customer service. I probably looked like I was leading the IT effort, but in truth, I was being pulled along by the demands of others. Ironically, I love technology but was miserable in my job. My self-image is that I am a thinker, someone with creativity who can innovate. That is where I am happiest. Staying in a reaction mode made my job tedious and unsatisfying."

This individual was in the field he loved (technology) but felt unsatisfied because he was not connected to his need to think at a higher level. His solution was to start his own consulting company so that he could respond to the needs of clients with thorough analysis and his own ideas about what would best serve the client.

"The difference between being a 'reactor' versus being a 'responder' is huge," he observes, "because I am able to not only use my skills, but also my brain. I thought I was doing my best at my former job but now I see that this disconnect pushed me downward so that I was not able to do my best. As I look back I realize that I probably was not a great employee, and certainly not a good boss, because I was so unfulfilled. Connecting my career to me was the best move ever."

Another friend of mine, an administrator in higher education, experienced the same kind of feelings.

"There was a crisis every day," he says. "If I solved the crisis I was just doing my job. If the crisis could not be resolved to someone's satisfaction then it was my fault. There were no victories—ever! I view myself as a builder, as someone who can see where things can be made better. My job never allowed me to get out of trenches and do what I do best and enjoy most."

This individual moved from higher education into corporate business development. His new role allows him to "keep improving the company's development process. It's all about thinking about how to change what we do so we can be better. It's a focus of the company so we are always collaborating, experimenting, and building. I'm in heaven. The result is that I am performing at a level at which even I did not know I was capable."

A few years ago a woman who had attended one of my CEO seminars made a significant career change. A month after the seminar, she resigned in order to work in a lower paying position for an organization that provides meals to the homeless.

IT IS YOUR JOB AS LEADER TO INSTILL LOYALTY IN YOUR COLLEAGUES AND EMPLOYEES. THIS IS ACCOMPLISHED BY FORMING AS MANY POSITIVE PERSONAL RELATIONSHIPS AS POSSIBLE.

"I realized after the seminar that I was a competent CEO but that I was hardly an engaged one," she says. "The title meant that I was the top dog, the salary meant I was more than comfortable on the financial front, and the position meant I was successful in my career. Yet, I was unhappy. During the seminar we discussed connecting who we are with what we do and that's when it became obvious that I was not connected at all. I have strong personal values that were constantly challenged at work and a service mentality that was never satisfied. My new position gives me so much more happiness and I am so much more engaged in the work because, well, it isn't work anymore. It's a joy."

Connecting the job to ourselves is an essential element of leadership, productivity, and personal happiness.

Leadership is about relationships.

TRUE LEADERS GRASP THAT RELATIONSHIPS DRIVE LOYALTY AND PRODUCTIVITY. It is your job as leader to instill loyalty in your colleagues and employees. This is accomplished by forming as many positive personal relationships as possible.

Leadership is a call to adapt to a world that has changed significantly in the last decade and has changed enormously in the last twenty years. This is not your father's workplace. This is a high-speed environment that requires we know who we are and how we apply our true selves to the tasks at hand. That's a requirement in a world that recognizes people productivity is most often based on two factors: (1) relationships with the boss/leader, and (2) employees receiving satisfaction from the job beyond salary and rewards.

This is important, says Bob Nelson, president of Nelson Motivation, Inc., a management and training firm. According to Nelson, "Employees today are no longer loyal to organizations as much as they are loyal to people."[2]

People desire a relationship with you. You can view these people as barriers to overcome, as in the command model, or as partners in the journey. If you want partners, you must relate to people in that fashion. As a

PEOPLE DESIRE A RELATIONSHIP WITH YOU. YOU CAN VIEW THESE PEOPLE AS BARRIERS TO OVERCOME, AS IN THE COMMAND MODEL, OR AS PARTNERS IN THE JOURNEY.

leader, you have many relationships with different pods of people as well as with individuals. The best leaders have an understanding of what moves people and pods to act in support of the corporate vision. Much of this book contains specific tools for forming quality relationships through well-defined values, a clearly articulated vision, and new communication skills.

Never doubt that those you lead are always examining your words and deeds for cues as to how you want them to speak and act. Through your own personal growth, you give permission to those around you to grow as well. Push yourself and you also push others to move to the next level. At the core of this sustained personal growth is your guiding set of principles and values. People know your principles because they observe you every day. Act out what you believe, do what you say, and do what you ask others to do. Your principles and values will enhance your relationships and therefore form your leadership.

L EADERSHIP REQUIRES A DAILY COMMITMENT TO THE ROLE SO THAT IT EXTENDS BEYOND MERELY PERFORMING OUR JOBS. The connection between the job and corporate values and goals is heightened by defining leadership as our vocation, and through that connection we increase our own productivity as well as the productivity of those around us. We become more attuned to our personal values, leadership style, and communication responsibilities to achieve more than previously possible. At the center, communication leadership is about relationships that align personal and corporate values. As we go forward, let's draw yet another clear distinction between communication leadership and command leadership. Command leadership seeks to intimidate or change people in order to achieve compliance. Communication leadership seeks to relate to people to achieve loyalty and commitment. The difference between those two concepts is the difference between happy and unhappy employees, healthy and dysfunctional organizational cultures, and successful and unsuccessful leaders.

CHAPTER TWO

★ ★ ★

PREPARE TO LEAD

White Hat Principles:

- ★ *Look beyond the obvious sources for tools and learning materials.*
- ★ *Take time away to recharge.*

THE MOVIE *JEREMIAH JOHNSON*, starring Robert Redford, tells the story of a man who dreams of achieving personal independence by becoming a mountain man, though he has little idea of what achieving this personal vision requires. He embarks on his journey one day by asking, "Where are the Rocky Mountains?" This inquiry exposes a weakness within his vision statement: He knows the name of his destination, but he has no idea where it is or how to get there. Corporate and personal vision statements often have the same weakness. We know we want to be "successful," "the best," and "the most respected," but we do not know what those terms actually mean. To be White Hat Leaders, we must know not only where we want to go but also how to recognize it when we arrive there.

Once in the mountains, Jeremiah finds he cannot keep a fire lit in the snow. He tries trapping for beaver but fails. He hunts but his rifle's range is too short and its bullet velocity too weak to fell large animals. While trying to catch fish from a mountain stream, Jeremiah finds himself before an Indian, a natural adversary who is carrying a long string of captured fish. In normal circumstances the intruding Jeremiah might be killed, but in this case the Indian's demeanor is one of contempt for the ineptness of the supposed mountain man. Jeremiah is not a worthy adversary, so the Indian is content to let Jeremiah die in wilderness.

The scene portrays a man who has no skills necessary to survive "out there." He is failing at a level that puts his life at risk. Two fortuitous events save him. (Luck also plays a part in business, but it is dangerous to rely on it. Relying upon luck to succeed is like relying upon the lottery to fund your retirement plan.) Jeremiah's first stroke of luck is the discovery of a dead mountain man still clutching a Henry .55 rifle. With this new and powerful survival tool, which Jeremiah should have known about and acquired before entering the mountains, he is able to down large game from a long distance. This necessary technology saves him in the short term.

A second stroke of luck is meeting an experienced mountain man nicknamed Bear Claw. Although now aware of his own vulnerability in the mountain, Jeremiah's arrogance forces him to brag about possessing skills that he does not possess, an assertion immediately challenged by the real mountain man who places Jeremiah in a cabin with a wild bear. The lesson makes its point. Bear Claw becomes a mentor to Jeremiah, teaching him how to hunt, trap beaver, and otherwise survive on the fringe of life, where resources are few and must be managed carefully. In time, Bear Claw teaches Jeremiah the skills to go beyond survival. Jeremiah learns to thrive.

PREPARATION IS THE ULTIMATE KEY TO SUCCEEDING AT ANYTHING. WHEN YOU DON'T PERSONALLY POSSESS THE SKILLS, KNOWLEDGE, OR TOOLS TO SUCCEED, IT IS UP TO YOU TO SEEK THESE THINGS.

Jeremiah entered the wilderness without a clear idea of the skills, knowledge, experience, or tools necessary to survive, much less to be successful. If not for the terrible fate of one mountaineer and the mentorship of another, he would have been doomed. His naïve notions about mountain life and his arrogance about his own limited abilities placed him in great danger. His safety and success were assured only after he opened himself up to use new tools and to accept the advice of others.

Those who rise to the challenges of business and life, meaning they succeed, were prepared before the challenge of leadership was thrust upon them, for there is no success as mountain man, carpenter, scientist, or leader if the tools and knowledge necessary for success are absent.

Preparation is the ultimate key to succeeding at anything. When you don't personally possess the skills, knowledge, or tools to succeed, it is up to you to seek these things. Most of us have seen firsthand how some people reject opportunities to learn more or to be mentored. Their perception is that seeking the knowledge and wisdom of others is a sign of weakness or, worse, incompetence. This is a defeatist approach to life in general and leadership skills specifically, for none of us can know it all—ever! We can only seek to know as much as possible, which creates a need to go to resources, people and otherwise, to find what will elevate us to another level of expertise. People without courage, humility, and a desire for excellence are thwarted because pride stunts their growth. Pride is an example of self-interest because it never allows the vulnerability necessary to open dialogue that results in learning.

> **PEOPLE WITHOUT COURAGE, HUMILITY, AND A DESIRE FOR EXCELLENCE ARE THWARTED BECAUSE PRIDE STUNTS THEIR GROWTH.**

As a person who seeks and encourages others to seek new information, I offer this observation: the more you know, the more you realize that you don't know much. This is a journey that should never end until we end.

Look beyond the obvious sources for tools and learning materials.

ONE OF MY CLOSEST FRIENDS ONCE CHASTISED ME FOR READING TOO MANY BUSINESS BOOKS. I scoffed at him because, after all, as a businessman and business consultant, I need to keep current with the latest research and theories.

That's fine, he'd say, but you will never "get game" until you appreciate that there are interrelationships among disciplines that can enrich your business level. Turn the business concepts upside down and see what new lessons fall out, he said. Then he handed me *Ethics for the New Millennium* by the Dalai Lama. I opened my mind and read it—and I found it full of valuable morsels that I could re-form into good business practices, even though many of the principles are a thousand years old.

It was from this experience that I became aware that answers exist in numerous, often unconventional, places, so I went exploring and haven't stopped. The journey has been great, exposing me to philosophies and techniques that apply directly to business, but that cannot be found in the latest treatise from a world-famous business guru.

I find that communication books, including some rather dry, graduate-level textbooks, are a gold mine of concepts that I can apply on a personal and professional level. Anthropology books and articles offer new insights into the impact of culture on an organization and help identify strengths and weaknesses within an organization's culture. Some of the best information is now evolving from theologians who are pursuing new paradigms in a postmodern world. Ron Mortoia's *Morph* is actually written for a religion-centered audience but contains great insights from secular authors as well as the theology community.

Business books remain a staple of my reading diet, though, with Jim Collins (*Built to Last* and others) emerging as a favorite author. Collins is now lecturing on the theology circuit as well as the business circuit, so he too recognizes the transference of ideas from one area to another. Magazines such as *Fast Company* and *Business 2.0* seem to always have at least one bit of information that I can use in lectures and in life. *Harvard Business Review* is a mine strewn with golden nuggets.

★ ★

IMPLEMENTATION:
Make time to read, and read diverse material.

The reading resources available are worthless if they are not used. Yes, you have a busy schedule and so does everyone else. Others find the time so you can find the time. If this remains problematic for you then place it in this context. If you cannot lead yourself, how in the heck can you lead others?

Make time to read books based on sound principles, whether in communication, philosophy, management, psychology, or theology. Hit the Net and search different subjects to find web articles that are often as intriguing as the newest business best seller.

You will certainly limit your vision for the future if you restrict yourself to reading trade magazines, although these are valuable to the mechanics of your business. I continue to read trades in several industries, including financial services, health, manufacturing, and philanthropy, to stay atop trend lines and to discover the new service or quality technique that works. Articles on evolving demographics are early detectors for trends that will impact your way of doing business in the future. The bottom line for leaders and would-be leaders is that, in the new century, knowledge of your industry alone is no longer sufficient. The mosaic nature of our culture requires a broad knowledge base to be able to relate, connect, and react to others.

Today's leader has to possess awareness of communication concepts, motivational psychology, and organizational culture as a baseline, or "Jacks to open," as one of my poker-playing colleagues likes to say.

★ ★

IMPLEMENTATION: *Ask for wisdom.*

Recall from the movie example that Jeremiah rejected help from Bear Claw by claiming skills he did not actually possess, because admitting this weakness would make him look inferior. This attitude remains with us. There is nothing wrong with going to others for guidance, but some people feel it is beneath them. These are the people you will pass as you climb the leadership ladder. White Hat leaders do not hesitate. They know the value of collaboration.

Ask those you respect, but who operate in a field different from yours, where they go to find information and to grow as leaders. Perhaps they have a favorite seminar that opened their eyes to new concepts, or a favorite author who inspired personal improvement.

These people are good at what they do for a reason. Ask them what they think, how they process information, and how they lead. What personal experiences do they possess that you can use and share with others?

I have a friend who, after I indicated interest in what she reads and thinks, now shares books and articles on a regular basis. She also engages me in lively discussions about her newest idea or a concept she discovered at a meeting. She's mentoring me in a most positive way, even though that is not her intent. The simple act of engaging in dialogue on subjects that pertain to our lives introduces new information that forces me to process what I am hearing and attempt to migrate this information to my experiences. You need at least one friend who performs this service for you.

The questions you ask do not need to be specific. In fact, general questions are best because they open the discussion to a wide range of possibilities.

I once asked a colleague, "How do leaders get better every day?" The question sounds simple, but the possible answers are infinite. His response was, "Ask. Then shut up and listen. Even better, hear." And then? "Ask another question." And then? "Ask the person to apply the answer to a real-world situation so you know how to use the answer in your business, or in your life, or both."

This is an essential element of the learning process; it is not enough to ask—you must also know how to apply the answer to your situation. Never fall into the trap of thinking knowledge is the ultimate answer. *Application* is the ultimate answer.

IMPLEMENTATION:
Create a feedback mechanism inside your business.

Ask employees what they think about actions taken as well as actions being considered. How has a past decision worked out? What could have been done to improve both the decision making and implementation process? This may be difficult at first because employees may not think you want a sincere answer. Initially, you will often hear what they think you want to hear. Repetition is the key to successful implementation of feedback. Over time, they will understand the sincerity of your request. When possible, act on the feedback and tell the person who offered it that you listened to what he or she said.

The ultimate beauty of this approach is that you will create an open process of dialogue that no longer requires you to ask the questions. This results from your giving permission to your staff to collaborate with you in creating better work methods. Achieving open dialogue is a sign that you have developed a highly positive culture that understands the importance of cooperation to reach common goals. Employees tend to be exceptionally happy in open dialogue cultures and equally loyal to the leader who encourages it. Conflict is largely absent from such cultures; people learn how to couch issues in impersonal terms and without blame because the focus is upon improvement rather than pointing fingers.

The validity of this concept was again made apparent during the writing of this book when an outsider and stranger (the editor provided by the publisher) began to rework what I had devoted a year to writing. This could have created a contentious relationship. Instead, it became a highly collaborative venture during which ideas were offered, rejected, and sometimes just laughed at without a moment of conflict. The reason for this delightful experience is that Lisa Anderson (editor) and the author removed ego from the process and focused on outcome. Lisa's genuine interest in the book and the enthusiasm she inserted into the process made her an ideal partner.

That is the work culture all of us would like to have, and it can be achieved in any venue by a similar approach. Self-interest inserts "I" into the picture when the reality is that all work is about "us." The observation was made earlier that people can be perceived as partners or barriers. Great leaders make their employees partners.

All of this is too soft, you may think, too philosophical to be considered meaningful. James Champy, chairman of Perot Systems Consulting and author of *X-Engineering the Corporation*, would disagree.

"Who would you follow into battle: the manager who spouts the vision thing, reads from the company's press releases, and feigns passion as the ship is sinking? Or, the manager—a smart one, of course—who displays empathy, understands how his behavior affects success and failure, and is open to discovering the truth? The latter hidden qualities are those that lead to sustained greatness."[1]

Those who believe that self development, communication skills, and culture analysis and response are soft skills are missing the point. These are hard skills because they result in hard numbers, such as numbers related to productivity, return on investment, and profit. Skills that positively impact these areas are necessary, and that is the definition of "hard skill."

★ ★

Good leaders know when to take time away to recharge.

PART OF PREPARING TO LEAD IS RECOGNIZING WHEN TO STEP AWAY TO RECHARGE. Most of us have experienced the benefits of taking time away from the office (or family) for a few days, then returning with new energy and a better perspective.

Stepping away allows us to work through issues and problems without the stress induced by a sense of urgency. It is usually in these moments of relaxation that we generate objective solutions. We must go away to return with clarity.

Going away is a difficult task for workaholics (I know because I am one). But the fact that we are workaholics means we must be disciplined enough and courageous enough to give ourselves this downtime. The reality is that workaholics have the best opportunity to step back because we inflict most of the extra workload ourselves. We can give ourselves nights and weekends if we stop confusing tasking with working.

Those who feel task saturated are the very people who need to step away most.

Self-inflicted task saturation is the result of either not having qualified support staff to whom to delegate tasks, or not having the willingness to delegate to staff.

Leaders must have time to think or they will likely forfeit their ability to lead. Task saturation causes us to react rather than respond. Reaction is a mechanical, almost involuntary reflex to events. It comes from the primal areas of the brain and does not involve real thought. Response is initiated from the cognitive regions of the brain. Reaction is normal for the task-saturated person; response comes from the leader who makes certain to allocate time for cognitive consideration.

One of my mentors gave me these instructions: always take vacation and holidays, and give yourself some quiet time during the week, including weekends. His summary statement remains with me: "You must disengage in order to truly engage."

★ ★

IMPLEMENTATION: *Determine if you have time to disengage.*

If you still think you do not have time to disengage, perform a simple exercise. First, examine the issues that keep you engaged. Are they urgent tasks or tasks that are simply important? If they are not urgent, you have time to disengage. Second, are these tasks that others should be able to perform as part of their jobs? If they are, delegate so people can have ownership of the work and its outcome. If you cannot delegate the tasks, answer the question, "Why not?" More than likely it is because you do not have the right people on staff.

★ ★

P REPARING TO LEAD IS ONE OF THE FIRST MAJOR STEPS TO BECOMING A WHITE HAT LEADER. It defines the quality of the foundation, so as with any foundation, it must be set before anything else is built upon it. Reading this section is not enough. These steps must be implemented and experienced, then applied to real-world situations. No one absorbs all this in one moment—it is a building process. Attaining each successive level of achievement requires effort.

One of my friends told me about an instance when his son was upset after a disastrous experience from the free throw line during a youth league basketball game. The father made this observation to his son: "You understand the game because you watch it. You understand the mechanics because you've been coached. But when I say you should go outside and practice free throws, you tell me you don't want to practice. All your knowledge of the game won't help you make those shots. You have to practice it before you can deliver when the game is on the line."

This is valuable advice to all of us. We have to put the principles into practice or we cannot succeed.

Once you have embraced and begun using the principles, you can teach others by suggestion, as well as by example, to **LEADERS MUST HAVE TIME TO THINK OR THEY WILL LIKELY FORFEIT THEIR ABILITY TO LEAD.** do the same. This leads to improved leadership skills not only of your staff but also of your supervisors. It can be as simple as asking your staff members to list their personal values, creating a value system for your office, division or company, and bringing in articles for employees to read and suggesting books. By doing these things you foster a highly beneficial common belief system and you prompt discussion that sets a strong foundation for future collaboration opportunities.

What you are really doing is establishing a positive culture in your workplace because people are learning to connect who they are with what they do, finding out more about each other, sharing interests, developing positive ways of dealing with each other, and learning how to make decisions that are consistent with the value system.

CHAPTER THREE

★ ★ ★

TRAITS OF EFFECTIVE LEADERS

White Hat Principles:

* ★ *Great leaders have courage.*
* ★ *Great leaders promote shared vision.*
* ★ *Great leaders leverage reality.*
* ★ *Great leaders have values.*
* ★ *True leaders operate with integrity.*

THERE ARE A MYRIAD OF BOOKS AND SEMINARS ON LEADERSHIP. Distill them all into a chapter and they will arrive at basically the same place. Great leaders have certain key traits, all of which are adaptable. While the traits remain constant, the methods and decisions of the leader show a healthy flexibility in a changing world.

Great leaders have courage.

ARISTOTLE ONCE WROTE THAT THE MOST IMPORTANT HUMAN TRAIT IS COURAGE, because without it, nothing else will happen. You can't achieve anything until you are willing to take the risk.

As a business owner and former member of a college faculty, I often appear at campus symposiums of various subjects, many of which involve entrepreneurship. The seminars generally follow the same pattern: the panelists make their perfunctory presentations and then we open for questions from students. Inevitably, a student looking for the ultimate shortcut will ask, "What is the *one* thing that is required to be a successful entrepreneur?"

The first panelist will respond that the answer is the great idea, the one that makes you different and better than the competition or the one that opens new markets. Heads will nod in agreement.

The second panelist usually disagrees. The idea is worthless without funding, he will say. There are a lot of great ideas out there but finding the start-up financing is very difficult. No idea gets off the ground unless you have the money to push the idea from concept to reality. And again heads will nod.

SIGMUND FREUD WROTE THAT THE DEFINITION OF PSYCHOSIS IS LIMITING OUR LIVES SO AS TO AVOID ANXIETY. BY THAT DEFINITION, WE ARE ALL PSYCHOTIC.

The third panelist will disagree. The most important thing is the ability to manage, she will say. You can have a great idea and funding, but without management skills, you will lose everything. Remember, three of every four businesses fail because of poor management skills.

And then it will be my turn. "You have to have the guts to take the risk," I say. Without guts, I tell the students, even with the best idea in the world, you will never seek the financing or be in a management position. Nothing good happens until you are willing to take the risk, and that, my friends, is where most businesses fail because the business never actually happens.

I cannot attribute the following statement to a specific person so let us attribute it to that great philosopher Anonymous: "It is the start that stops most people."

Think about this for a moment. You probably know someone who has two or three great ideas each year. He tells you about these ideas with wonderful enthusiasm. He can even outline how to make millions, or at least thousands, with this new idea. Yet, that person has never acted on a single one. No guts.

Why is it we cannot move forward, not only to start a business but also to lead a business? The reason is anxiety. Anxiety makes us create reasons not to act.

Sigmund Freud wrote that the definition of psychosis is limiting our lives so as to avoid anxiety. By that definition, we are all psychotic. Who doesn't hate facing an anxiety-ridden situation? Who among us has not avoided making a decision because of the anxiety associated with the decision? We all have bowed to anxiety at some point in our professional lives, even though we knew we should make a decision and act upon it.

You probably feel, as I do, that the most anxiety-filled and difficult action is firing someone. I know that behind that person is likely a family, perhaps dependent upon this person's financial and mental well-being. When we fire a person, the action often goes well beyond the person we remove from our organization. Nonetheless, we must, for the good of the organization, act. The reality is that we often know that this person needs to be fired months, even a year, before we get around to it, solid evidence that we feel anxiety and that anxiety paralyzes our actions. The pattern of behavior is basically the same for most of us.

After rationalizing and procrastinating, I arrive at the day when I think I can pull off this task I have dreaded. I arise in the morning and think, today I can do it. I chart my course and arrive at the office steeled for the event.

I can fire her first thing in the morning, I think, and get it out of the way. But wait—that's a terrible way to start one's day. Besides, this gives her all day to think about buying a gun. I cannot fire her first thing. I'll wait until mid-morning. No, that won't work because I have a meeting at 10:00 a.m. I know, I'll take her to lunch and fire her over a nice farewell meal in an informal setting. That won't work! What if she cries or yells? A public place is not a good option. No, I need to wait until the afternoon. But I told my spouse that I would run that errand this afternoon so that will not work either. I've got it—I'll fire her at closing time. But that would be terrible! How can you fire someone at the end of the day and send her home depressed?

You see what has happened. I have now gone through the entire day and avoided doing what must be done. Anxiety has led me to find reasons not to act. To make matters worse, the anxiety-filled situation remains, and in that is the irony attached to procrastination. The problem remains for another day, or month, or year.

★ ★

IMPLEMENTATION: *Teach yourself to go*
to the pain and go there quickly.

We have to make an internal value decision to go to the pain. Great leaders have an ability to do this. You can use one of many catch phrases: the negative is the imperative, deal with the bad stuff first, and so on. Whatever slogan you choose is fine; just create one that keeps you focused on dealing with anxiety-generating issues.

Teach yourself to go to the pain and go there quickly, because much of the anxiety we feel builds over time. Once we make the tough call, the anxiety is diminished if not totally dismissed. The faster we *act* on the decision, the better we feel. The core irony is that avoidance to diminish anxiety instead creates a continuing pattern of anxiety.

I work with an executive who uses a technique called "no regrets." Whenever he faces a significant issue of this nature he simply takes out a piece of paper and writes down all the possible negative results of the action he must take. Once the list is complete, he reviews it by saying out loud each item on the list. When he concludes, he says, "I make this decision with no regrets." This gives him the courage to act.

As the criticisms are voiced, he actually feels affirmed because he can say, "I knew you were going to say that." He sometimes removes the yellow sheet of paper from his desk drawer to display how eerily accurate he was in predicting the criticisms. People who see the list are almost always in awe and it supports his contention that the decision was reached through a thoughtful process.

No leader who wants to stay a leader can let anxiety rule her actions. Courage is necessary for leadership. Remember, a leader cannot be concerned with the applause meter.

Great visions are like great ideas. It takes courage to act upon them, as it takes courage to accomplish a myriad of small things in a business setting. Ideas and visions do not become reality without intentional implementation, and it takes courage to implement. Imagine Marco Polo without courage. Imagine Columbus without courage, or Gandhi, or Martin Luther King, Jr. If it weren't for courage, these names would be unknown to us. Bill Gates had courage enough to attack a vision that was as far-fetched in his youthful days as a vision to walk on the moon would have been in 1950.

Again we are led back to the principle of making leadership a vocation. Leadership guru Peter Koestenbaum sums it up this way in the February 2000 edition of *Fast Company*: "So how do you motivate people? Not with techniques but by risking yourself with a personal, lifelong commitment to greatness—by demonstrating courage."[1]

★ ★

Great leaders promote shared vision.

A COMMONLY TAUGHT AXIOM OF LEADERSHIP IS THAT LEADERS MUST BE VISION-ARIES. This is not true. Vision for an organization can come from anywhere within the organization, and probably should flow from several people in different areas of work. A vision that arises from within the organization is better because it is more likely to be universally embraced than one that comes from a single source at the top. Shared vision is always superior to single vision. A leader totally alone in his or her vision will find no followers.

Seizing vision as personal property has a way of reflecting a top-down leadership style that creates barriers to system-wide acceptance of the vision. This creates barriers to system-wide implementation of the vision. The people who want to own the employees, the work, and the credit are the ones who desire single ownership of vision. Good leaders, on the other hand, desire collaboration and positive association so they include others in the development process, create internal advocates, and use the buy-in of employees to help cast the vision.

How the vision is presented significantly impacts the willingness of employees to embrace the vision.

★ ★

IMPLEMENTATION: *Share the vision.*

Sharing the vision involves answering three questions: (1) Where are we going? (2) Why are we going there? (3) How do we get there?

Transferring the corporate vision to the many parts of the organization is often difficult. It requires digging deeper into the organization to make certain that all the parts are working collectively and collaboratively with common purpose. Common purpose does not require common roles, but roles at each employee level must directly relate to a common purpose. These common roles must be defined and reinforced over and over again, even to the point that you may think you said all you need to say as much as you need to say it. You will be wrong. Consistent performance is a by-product of consistent messaging. Focusing on the vision and its parts (where, why, how) maintains focus and commitment to the related tasks. The failure of any one department to roll out its contribution in a timely fashion negatively impacts achieving the vision.

> Consistent messages at all levels of an organization over a long period of time generate results. Jeanie Daniel Duck, author of *The Change Monster,* calls it "conversion through conversation."[2]
>
> We think of visioning as being a corporate-wide function, but that is not correct. The concept works the same in all areas. A vision can be cast for a division or even for an office of a few people.
>
>

WHERE ARE WE GOING?

Answering this question reveals to everyone the destination, or where the vision is taking the organization. Leaders should articulate vision in a way so that when you all arrive, you know you have arrived and have succeeded in the journey. Vague words and phrases such as "biggest," "best," "fastest growing," "most respected," and others of that nature are difficult to define. After all, how do you *really* know when you are the most respected company in your field? Without definition, the vision can never be attained, a frustrating condition for those challenged with making it happen.

WHY ARE WE GOING THERE?

The second step answers, "Why are we going there?" When employees know motive (why), they know the context for choosing the vision and therefore can do a better job for you. Motive is very important if we wish to motivate people to stay focused on a vision. Yet, despite its absolute importance to a successful outcome, the "why" question is the most neglected aspect of the visioning process.

Although visions should inspire, the vision alone will not produce the buy-in needed to achieve success. There must always be a reason for what we do, and it should be stated clearly and persuasively to everyone—or we will likely achieve less than we hoped.

When people understand there are good reasons for the vision, whether it solves a problem or produces a competitive advantage, they will fully engage in the process. Otherwise, they will ask questions in the hallways, offices, nooks, and crannies of your company. Even more devastating is that those employees, in the absence of a clear explanation from leadership, will make up answers to the questions. This subterranean discussion of what is happening inside the corporation can have a devastating impact on the visioning process.

Statements such as "I don't understand why we are doing this" indicate the staff is incapable of being fully committed and is likely creating its own explanation for the vision that is far from the truth. Immediate intervention is required when employees feel the vision and its parts are ambiguous.

HOW ARE WE GETTING THERE?

The third step answers the question, "How are we getting there?" A great tactical plan identifies important movement toward the vision. This is the response for achieving the vision, the steps to success, so to speak. Turn the discussion of vision into a verb rather than a noun. Vision is not something you have. Vision is something you do.

Too often, we create vision but avoid the drudgery of outlining what we will do to achieve the vision. We simply send people back to work, vision in hand, and expect them to figure out how they and their groups will respond. This approach often fails because results across working groups are uneven. Some groups will perform magnificently while others will flounder, never quite sure what they should do to contribute. People need to understand their relevance to the vision, as well as the relevance of the vision to them.

Each working group should have its own implementation plan in writing that outlines the specific steps to take and who is accountable for each step. Accountability is key, so name names. Add dates as well so that everyone works with a sense of urgency.

When you achieve milestones along the way, celebrate! Most visions take a long time to achieve, often too long to sustain without experiencing some success as you go. The microcosm is the example of a project. Projects have their own life span outside the beginning and end dates we place upon them because people have restricted attention spans. This is simply a fact of life. A project lasting more than six months begins to lose momentum as people become distracted with other tasks and tire of working on this monster that will not be subdued. Simply put, employees become fatigued.

For visions cast over years, how do you maintain momentum and staff engagement in the process? It is second nature for most of us to tire of an effort that takes a long time to implement. It is important that leaders define the shortest possible due date for its completion. Longer durations require more maintenance from the leadership in order to keep people energized and focused.

A good leadership approach is to celebrate milestones along the way. A great tactical plan identifies important movement toward the vision. When these points are reached, stop, reflect on where you are and where you are going, and enjoy the moment. Build specific achievements into the system so people will feel the progress and enjoy it.

A nonprofit organization had a vision to protect the lives and health of young people by fostering early detection of juvenile diabetes. This would be achieved by raising public awareness through the establishment of ten new community chapters in a year. This organization's vision had valuable sections to answer the where, why, and how questions. The vision stated where they were going (a public awareness campaign), why they were going there (to protect the lives and health of young people), and how to get there (by establishing ten new community chapters within a year).

Although the vision statement contained all the required elements, the central organization had a difficult time creating and implementing strategies that would achieve the desired outcome. This is not unusual, because vision statements do not achieve the level of involvement required for success without additional, specific information about the "how" question. The solution was to create a separate vision for each department that corresponded with what the organization wanted to achieve. For example, the marketing department needed to have a vision as to how to inform people in a way that encouraged volunteers. The events department needed a vision as to how it would use community outreach to do the same. The fund-raising area needed a vision that allowed it to identify funding sources and to write proposals that met the funding requirements of those sources. Finally, the administrative division needed a vision as to how it would locate facilities and recruit staff, should staff be necessary (volunteers can often serve staff functions). These visions were then redefined for each individual in these areas, so everyone knew what he or she needed to do in order to succeed as an organization. This application of the organization's vision more tightly defined how each department and person connected to the vision and the value each brought to the total effort.

The ten community chapters did not simultaneously appear, of course, which was a good thing. This gave the leadership an opportunity to organize a "grand opening" of each chapter. Each grand opening validated the work of the organization and the staff and provided hard evidence that there was progress toward attaining the vision.

★ ★

IMPLEMENTATION: *Place vision in the context of the listener rather than the presenter.*

Articulating the vision is very important and is one of the primary roles of a leader. When crafting a vision, be aware of the words you choose and the meanings they convey. Most of us spend too little time on craftsmanship. Words matter.

A university researcher planned to show three test groups a videotape of an accident involving two cars.

To the first test group he said, "I am going to show you a tape of two cars *hitting* each other." To the second group he said, "I am going to show you a tape of two cars *colliding* together." He told the third group, "I am going to show you a tape of two cars *smashing* together." All groups watched the same tape.

The first group believed the cars were going at under 15 miles per hour. The second group, after being told the cars collided, believed the cars were traveling at 30 miles per hour. The third group, having been told that the cars smashed together, offered that the cars were traveling at 40 miles per hour. Some in the group reported seeing flying glass. There was no flying glass.

They all viewed the same tape, so what changed their perception? One word.

Messaging within vision is of extreme importance because context of messaging is a powerful leadership tool for swaying opinion. Choosing the right word is always about the context of the person(s) receiving the message. Sending messages in context is discussed further in Chapter 7.

★ ★

Great leaders leverage reality.

WHITE HAT LEADERS CARRY WITH THEM A DOSE OF REALITY AT ALL TIMES. Purely visionary leaders can take an organization into oblivion by constantly grabbing onto new ideas and changing course to implement a different vision than the one last week. A leader who is totally visionary is a dangerous being, indeed.

Likewise, a purely reality-based leader is not a leader at all because she tends to create rut-oriented organizations that move only when the numbers say they should move—a rare occurrence, to be honest. Besides, when the numbers dictate a move it is probably already too late.

Reality-based leaders tend to kill creativity by asking questions such as, "If this is such a good idea, why isn't someone else doing it?" Or, "That sounds too expensive for us so why would we even bother?" Or, "Why change what we're doing when it works?" These responses kill creativity because no staff will offer ideas when consistently faced with them.

The classic declarative from a reality-based leader is, "If it ain't broke, don't fix it." Given that no organization has ever achieved perfection, how is it possible for it never to be in need of performing better? The real message sent by this statement is, "This is as good as it gets"—not the message a leader wants to send.

Pure reality-based leaders are as dangerous as pure vision-based leaders in that they limit possibilities. Great leaders have a little bit of both so they can balance themselves and their organizations. The most effective leaders can face and understand the bare, brutal facts, but do not allow the facts to limit vision or possibility.

The vision of the previously mentioned nonprofit may not have been achievable, particularly under the time frame, had leadership diffused the work of the staff by introducing new visions. Leaders sometimes make visions ambiguous by not understanding this reality of employee behavior.

IMPLEMENTATION: *Use reality to temper vision.*

Reality tempers vision so your organization does not make decisions without the balance that comes from knowledge of your environment and the conditions of your organization.

A consultant spent several months of one year working with a domestic organization to develop a global communications strategy, a vision of outreach that was far beyond what the organization had previously achieved. Communication was a key element in securing much-needed outside funding to support its scientific and humanitarian work, as well as to distribute the valuable findings that resulted from work in the field. The management gave the consultant instructions to create the best plan for accomplishing specified goals. He was told not to worry about the condition of the communications area, which, everyone agreed, was in shambles.

As the consultant interviewed, researched, and ultimately began writing the communication plan, he became haunted by the feedback received from different areas of the organization. There was no confidence in the communications group to successfully implement any plan, as there was, in essence, no communications department. Rather, media relations was in one department, publishing in another, and web in yet a third. Collectively, the communication areas were terribly understaffed and underfunded, to the point that people with marginal media experience were routinely pulled in from various technical areas to write releases, reports, and books, and to coordinate media.

The consultant was faced with a leader who delivered a vision of worldwide coverage for this organization—without taking a good look at the organization and staff that would be asked to undertake this significant effort.

As he worked through the plan, the consultant began to add chapters that disclosed the need for more money, new positions, and a significant reorganization of staff so that communication sections would combine in one department inside a single division.

The plan caused huge internal turmoil. Only one division was willing to give up its hold on one of the units. Heads of the respective communication units began power struggles to become the director of this proposed new department. However, the CEO told the consultant that the plan was good. "We will do many of the things you suggest," was the follow-up. And then he threw the lightning bolt.

"The reality is that we cannot implement an international plan," he said grimly. "As you point out, we do not have the staff to make this happen in a professional way. We simply cannot change too drastically what we have as it will upset too many people and create staff problems, as you have already seen. This is a good vision for us. We simply do not have the people and resources to make it happen."

The visionary leader in the office was revealed as a reality-based leader in life. And, as with many reality leaders, he was anxiety averse. There were too many challenges that he would not accept. Unfortunately, it was those challenges that doomed the vision from the beginning.

Many leaders so desire to be visionary that they jump at the chance to do something exciting, thinking of the barriers only after the process is launched. This CEO did not balance the reality of his situation with the vision that inspired him. Until he made his list of anxieties and said,

"No regrets," he should have avoided hiring a consultant.

Use reality as a test to temper vision. As a leader, you need to be able to thrive within the tension between vision and reality. In addition, let reality help form vision. Every vision must begin with recognition of where you are versus where you want to be. Your reality may be an organization fraught with pressures from competition, a changing market, or a dysfunctional internal culture. In this context, reality is a grain of sand inside your otherwise comfortable oyster, irritating to the extent that a response is desirable, maybe even necessary.

"I like where we are now," said one manager, "but we'll die if we are still here in five years because each technology wave changes the relationship with our customer."

This manager's reality is that his company needs to constantly move toward the next great innovation. To be behind in technology means the competition has an opportunity to be more responsive to the market. This person rose from manager to leader when he realized the only recourse is to keep making pearls—in his case, new visions that force forward momentum in an organization that could go on cruise control for a few years, enjoying its present success.

Unless your organization enjoys a monopoly it must always be in state of metamorphosis, evolving at a controlled rate. Reality, then, both balances vision as well as launches vision.

In both cases a leader becomes an agitator by upsetting people he must hold back and pushing people who will not go forward. The idea of leader as agitator repels many people, including those in leadership positions. Get over it. The type of agitation required for success varies with circumstances. Nonetheless, in forms great and small, agitation is always required for effective leadership.

★ ★

Great leaders have values.

FUTURIST LEONARD SWEET EMPHASIZES THE IMPORTANCE OF THIS PRINCIPLE WHEN HE OBSERVES, "In the global world of business, the most distinguishing quality of a leader has become the ability to lead through values. Value setting has replaced goal setting as the primary task of leadership."[3]

PERSONAL VALUES

WE BRIEFLY TOUCHED UPON PERSONAL VALUES IN CHAPTER 1. It's important that we delve deeper into this subject as it is a main driver of leadership success. On a personal level, the White Hat leader must be able to articulate the values he possesses. It is amazing how values, when exhibited to staff, flow throughout the organization, raising the level of performance in each division, department, and office. People sense and see these traits in action, copy them, and thereby multiply the positive impact on the organization.

Employees across all organizations, when asked what key trait they desire in a leader, respond that integrity is the most important. Without integrity, leaders may have compliant employees but never committed ones. The difference between the two is significant and impacts organizational success.

Integrity reaches into the heart of the leadership. We all want the people with whom we associate to treat us with integrity, but it is paramount in a leader. A leader without personal integrity is likely a leader without true followers. Your staff may listen and obey, but this is far from following.

Two examples from my own life demonstrate the effects of leadership integrity—or lack thereof.

The first example involves Toby Robertson, a man who has made a life in broadcasting. During the year when I worked as assistant news director at a radio station, Toby was my boss and was the primary news anchor.

WITHOUT INTEGRITY, LEADERS MAY HAVE COMPLIANT EMPLOYEES BUT NEVER COMMITTED ONES. THE DIFFERENCE BETWEEN THE TWO IS SIGNIFICANT AND IMPACTS ORGANIZATIONAL SUCCESS.

As a college student working in a new profession, I made my share of mistakes. Toby never raised his voice—instead, he used every mistake as an opportunity to teach his young assistant how to improve at his job.

Toby also was, and still is, a man of great integrity. He never lied or pushed the truth even a little. His matter-of-fact, forthright personality meant that he offered ready criticism and ready praise. He'd tell me that he would work me into a broadcast, or promise to give me a major opportunity to shine, and he delivered every time. He promised me that when he left, I would get his job, a commitment he did not have to make. When he resigned to take a job at a television station, he went to our station manager and told him there was no need for a search because their man was already on staff. The station manager believed him because he, too, knew Toby as a man of integrity.

I always knew where I stood with him, and the result was a committed employee, absolutely loyal to Toby Robertson.

The second example is entirely different. I consider the man involved as a mentor because he taught me how *not* to be a leader. For that reason, his real name will not be used.

"Bill" headed a media division and was a man of many ideas, although most were lost in the clutter of busywork that he generated due to his inability to prioritize. Even so, my first year with Bill was exciting because he was always innovating. This man was trapped in the vision mode, which kept everyone hopping and haggard. About halfway through my first year, the staff gathered to make a pact that no directions from Bill would be acted upon for twenty-four hours so that we would not waste time starting projects today that would be replaced tomorrow by a new project.

During the second year, the patterns I barely noticed during the first became more apparent. Bill used promises to bend people to his will. "If you will take on this extra assignment, I will reward you at raise time," he might say. But no such reward would happen.

"This is a big project and I am giving it to you so you can show off what you can do," he would say. But when the big project came to fruition, Bill would take all the credit.

> BY THOUGHTFULLY APPLYING INTEGRITY TO EVERY DECISION, YOU CREATE A TRACK RECORD THAT COMMUNICATES HOW YOU ARE LIKELY TO RESPOND TO ANY GIVEN IDEA OR EVENT.

Staff would meet with Bill one-on-one and then compare notes to discover Bill was telling each individual something different. No one could possibly know the truth. No matter how hard we tried, the staff was unable to ratchet up the commitment needed to do what we were capable of doing. We were merely compliant, providing what was asked and not a bit more. The energy that produces ideas and high quality of work was gone. Morale dove and résumés flew out the door.

Leadership often involves the use of symbols. Bill's everyday approach to business symbolized an absence of integrity, which resulted in his losing the ability to inspire his people to work at maximum capacity.

One of the core outcomes of integrity is consistency of leadership. By thoughtfully applying integrity to every decision, you create a track record that communicates how you are likely to respond to any given idea or event, and that your responses will fall well within established value systems you have set for yourself and your organization.

Falling back on your value system creates consistency. As one executive put it, "It's right or wrong—people living in the gray areas are in trouble." The gray area creates ambiguity for you and for those who work with you. Consistency creates a team that watches out for you and suggests what you wish to accomplish.

In their book *The Integrity Advantage*, Adrian Gostick and Dana Telford quote Wayne Sales of Canadian Tire as saying, "Making a decision usually takes one of two roads. One is doing the right thing. To take the other road, you have to sit back and spin a story around the decision or action you are taking."[4]

Take the other road too often and you have introduced ambiguity into your culture because you sometimes do the "right thing" and sometimes you do not.

The Integrity Advantage offers another appropriate quote, this time from Diane Peck of Safeway. She says, "People who have integrity are consistent in what they say and do. People with integrity have this consistency, this predictability, this believability."[5]

Inconsistency creates hidden agendas and "butt-covering" actions, as people attempt to protect themselves from the unknown created by the leader's inconsistent behavior. This counter-productive response is understandable because the unknown frightens all of us.

When you consistently apply your values, style of leadership, communication, and decisions, you create an atmosphere of productivity that flows from each employee knowing what is expected and allowable. Employees who constantly ask permission to act are employees who do not know what is allowable and are therefore fearful to do what they deem to be right. The word "fearful" is accurate because these people are afraid to make a decision for fear of being wrong. In this environment, the leader loses access to the creativity and problem-solving skills present in the employee. Associated with this is a leader who loses much of his own work time to meetings with staff who feel a need to gain permission for even the simplest and most obvious of activities.

★ ★

IMPLEMENTATION: *Describe your values.*

The first step to reaching this uplifting state of being is formulating a clear picture of who you are and what you represent so that an employee can create points of association with you—a shared area that results in one or more common bonds.

Begin by writing down five of your values as a person. These are values you live and work by. Following each, write a short description of an event that illustrates you not only believe this item but also live it. If you find you cannot pinpoint any events, you may not have ever exhibited this value so you should reevaluate your position. Is this really you or is it someone you would like to be? Remember, it is permissible to work toward defining a "new you" by identifying values you want to adopt and to begin working toward that goal.

There is nothing wrong with being unable to write the description—it simply means that you are still developing as a person and leader. If your value statement is a goal rather than a reality, write a description of when you could have used this value in the past, or when you envision using it in the future. Remember, writing down your values cements the list in your psyche so that you can draw upon it when you actually need to apply the values.

After each description write an impact statement. This is the outcome of applying the value.

Here is an example from a seminar participant.

VALUE: INTEGRITY

EVENT: A member of my staff had a run of bad luck. His car needed unexpected costly repairs. A storm had blown down a tree in his yard but insurance did not cover the removal of the tree. A water pipe burst in his yard and had to be repaired. The total amount he spent on these events reached thousands of dollars. He was in desperate need of cash. I knew he would soon be inquiring about his bonus which, unfortunately, he would not receive (more bad luck). I wanted to avoid the conversation because I knew he needed that bonus. It would have been easy to avoid him and just let the absence of a bonus check deliver the bad news. Instead, I went to his office and closed the door. My message, as gently as I could deliver it, was that there would be no bonus, but I would work closely with him for the next six months to make certain that he reached all his goals for the next bonus period. In the meantime, if I could find ways to legitimately give him overtime I would make that happen.

IMPACT: Although I was unable to give him a bonus, this honest and caring approach seemed to take the sting out of the news. In fact, he was grateful that I came to his office and acknowledged his troubles. In addition, because I told him well in advance of the official announcements about bonuses (instead of waiting until the last minute) he had additional time to arrange a favorable loan that covered his debts until the next bonus period. I am happy to report he earned a bonus six months later that helped him pay off the loan ahead of schedule.

Here is a second real-world example, also from a workshop.

VALUE: TRANSPARENCY

EVENT: My company is reorganizing and that has all the negative connotations one can possibly imagine when the word is used in an "all-staff" meeting. The groans were loud and long. Of course, everyone felt exposed, so you could feel the paranoia in the room. After the all-staff gathering, I brought all my division staff into a large conference room and gave the much too long speech about how we really should not be worried, which generated more groans. So, I made a promise that everything impacting our division would be on the table for everybody to see, and that I personally promised to discuss each planned "reorg" in advance so the staff could have input. If I needed to champion our division, I would do it.

IMPACT: The rumors and backbiting that have become an everyday occurrence in other divisions have never happened in mine because my people know what is going on and why. Sometimes—I should say often—the staff offers suggestions that improve the reorganization process. I wish I could say I was brilliant but the reality is that people just wanted to know what was going on, why, and how they would be impacted by the flurry of decisions. I'm going to admit here that I had no idea that this was the smart thing to do. It just seemed right. A bunch of my fellow directors thought I was crazy. Now they wish they had done what I did. Do we have arguments? You bet we do. But every single person in my division loves this experience, and the reorganization that has already ruined the relationship of some directors with their staffs strengthens my relationship with mine. It was a great lesson learned.

★   ★

True leaders operate with integrity.

INTEGRITY REQUIRES BOTH COURAGE AND HUMILITY. Humility is a first cousin to taking responsibility, and it is also a by-product of courage. It takes courage to be vulnerable.

White Hat leaders operate with a degree of humility, because this is what allows them to take responsibility for all that happens on their watch and to force decision making outside the gray areas. Leaders are easier to follow when they do not operate with butt-covering, swashbuckling arrogance. For example, the most respected leaders of the most successful companies rarely ever attribute the success of the organization to their leadership; they most often give the credit to employees, timing, or even "dumb luck."

In 1927, T.S. Eliot wrote a profound truth: "Humility is the most difficult of all virtues to achieve; nothing dies harder than the desire to think well of oneself."[6] It is equally true that we desire others to think well of us. Humility requires us to be vulnerable, a condition none of us enjoy.

An example of a lost opportunity to demonstrate humility involves the aftermath of Hurricane Katrina in the fall of 2005, a disaster that brought out some of the best and worst of human nature.

One organization put itself and its employees in harm's way in order to provide essential services during and after the hurricane. These efforts received well-earned praise. Although many employees were involved in this effort, the press covered one person, the man most identified with the organization's heroic efforts. The media interviewed this person on numerous occasions, and he accepted the accolades on a personal level while summarily failing to applaud in specific or general terms the contributions of others.

Amazingly, when asked why he failed to promote the organization and its employees, his response was, "The reporters asked to speak to me." Apparently, he believed this gave him permission to narrow the focus of the spotlight to himself.

Every one of us can show humility, even those gargantuan icons such as Isaac Newton, who remarked that his work rested upon the shoulders of giants. We so rarely see humility in this world of self-advancement that we find it significant when it does appear.

One corporate executive remarked about his embarrassment when his staff gave him a "We love our boss" award at a party. This outpouring of affection was complemented by extemporaneous speeches from the staff about how each one felt positively impacted by simply being around the executive.

"I actually cried," he told me. "They must think I am a wimp."

Not so, explained one of the staff. "He's such a humble man. We just loved him more."

HONESTY

Honesty is so easily forgotten in any number of everyday decisions because hedging against the reality is sometimes easier than facing the reality.

I once was hired to fire several people because the management team did not have the courage to do so. Several of the employees on my blacklist were fully capable, were performing well in their jobs, and had no record of actionable misbehavior or incompetence. The reason for the termination had nothing to do with performance; rather, the new management didn't favor them and wanted to hire its own hand-chosen people.

There is nothing inherently wrong with management building its own team. The wrong here is that these people were being treated in a completely dishonest manner. The managers told the employees that they had brought in an independent consultant to provide an objective review and make recommendations. Remember that the independent consultant's mission was to fire these people.

Frankly, I could not in good conscience execute the contract as written and verbalized. Instead, I called in each person and asked how he or she felt about his or her future with the company. Every person indicated that he or she had little faith in the new management team, which had already begun using strong-arm control tactics to initiate change. A few employees openly discussed the downward spiral of the corporate culture. I gave them this summary: you can leave on the company's timetable or you can leave before three months are up. They had their window—three months to exit on their own. Fortunately, each found a job and resigned rather than being fired.

The company executives could have used the same approach. Instead, the company chose to be dishonest and hid behind its notion of acceptable integrity by announcing an independent review that did not exist.

Another example of dishonesty wrapped in integrity is similar and often repeated. Most companies perform periodic reviews of their employees. Designed to be an integrity tool, the reviews are usually vague numerical pronouncements on the performance of the employee during a certain period, usually quarterly or annual. Almost without fail the supervisor will rate the employee high, even though the supervisor is less than thrilled with the person's performance. This happens in part because the supervisor has no courage to look the employee in the eye and verbalize issues that should transfer to the scorecard. The disservice to the employee is obvious.

You may know firsthand an employee with a folder full of stellar reviews who was summarily sacked, blindsided by the termination because the employee believed he was performing the job in an acceptable manner. The employee had no opportunity to change his behavior or improve competence because he had no warning that the supervisor was unhappy.

The evaluation system is in place to provide integrity in the relationship between the employee and supervisor, but the use of the evaluation is often dishonest.

★ ★

IMPLEMENTATION: *Balance humility and courage.*

Integrity has two anchors: humility and courage. A leader must be humble enough to expose her values and take the heat when necessary, which places her in a vulnerable position. The leader cannot function in this way if she is self-righteous and selfish. In addition, leaders must have the courage to be humble, a challenge inside most corporate boardrooms. Truth and honesty lie between these anchors. The foundation that supports all of these elements is a clearly articulated value system that keeps the leader pointed in the direction of integrity.

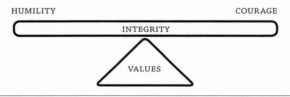

TAKING RESPONSIBILITY

In the early 1970s I created a mess when, as writer and narrator of a prerecorded syndicated radio show, I distributed a program that contained incorrect information. It was not partially wrong, it was entirely wrong. The first calls to the office came at 7:00 a.m.

By the time I arrived at the office at 8:00, the place was experiencing mass terror. The financial department was upset, the administration was furious, and all the cold fingers in the office were pointed at me.

The boss walked out of his office and signaled me to come inside for what I knew would be a farewell address. He peered over his glasses and asked, "Where'd you get the info?" I told him it came from two sources, one of which was published. "Did you run the copy by anyone?" he asked. Yes, I told him, I had run the copy by our usual fact checker. There was silence.

"You did what you could do," he said. "I'll handle it from here. Go to work."

I never met with the angry big guns that day—my boss did that dirty chore for me. He told them that I followed procedure, we were sorry, we'd do what we could do to salvage what was salvageable, and that we'd make no promises that mistakes would not be made again.

My boss was a true leader who took responsibility. I wonder if the rest of us would have done the same.

★ ★

IMPLEMENTATION: *Take responsibility for mistakes that occur under your leadership.*

Despite the fact that leaders encourage shared decision making, leaders always take responsibility for what happens inside their organizations. This is what people expect of a leader. No one can become a true leader until that lesson is learned.

John Kennedy took the hit for the Bay of Pigs because it happened on his watch, even though he did not plan it. The previous administration hatched and partially launched the plans. It was Kennedy, though, who went on national television and gave the mea culpa.

Bernie Ebbers, former CEO of WorldCom, took the opposite approach. Somehow this CEO built and managed a huge international organization without, he asserts, knowing what was going on. The financials were over his head, he argued, yet he headed mergers and acquisitions that created a global powerhouse of a company. Mr. Ebbers took all the credit—until the Feds knocked on his door.

Placing personal advancement over the corporate mission inevitably results in serious mistakes in judgment, perhaps even unintended mistakes. Yet people will make mistakes, deliberate or not (and I am giving Mr. Ebbers wide leeway here), when the focus is on self. For most of us, taking responsibility means backing up our people when they make mistakes. If you want to create loyal employees, protect them in bad times.

Personal advancement is an outcome, rather than a goal, of good leadership. Take care of the company. The personal glory will result. If you cannot buy into this concept then you probably do not possess the following value.

★   ★

Good leaders are transparent.

TRANSPARENCY IS A BY-PRODUCT OF BOTH COURAGE AND INTEGRITY AND INCLUDES THE CONCEPT OF HUMILITY. People do not have to agree with you to be a committed follower, but they do need to understand you.

Humans tend to guard themselves from the criticism of others. Transparency, therefore, often seems counter-intuitive because it challenges us to lay ourselves bare before others. Though it is not easy, it is an essential leadership value that is appreciated by others. Often, this trait distinguishes a leader from a dictator. It takes a strong sense of self-definition to be able to exhibit transparency.

Transparency means allowing others to view the process of decision making (perhaps even participating in the process), sharing the motive, and providing opportunity for evaluation by others.

Another facet of transparency requires that we tell the whole truth. Truth is sometimes different from honesty in that truth can be about telling partial truth, most of the truth, or omitting the truth.

Recently, I heard an executive asked a direct question: "Is there a plan to change the product line for our company? If there is, I need to know because I need to be looking for a job."

The executive responded that there was no plan to change the product line. That was the truth in that corporate executives had decided to change the product line but had not drafted the *plan* to execute the decision. The drafting of the plan would delay specific action for some time. It also meant that the employee, legitimately concerned about having a job, lost valuable time.

Was the executive lying? He rationalized that "technically" he had told the truth by answering the precise question, "Is there a plan?" Yet, he knew he was not answering the real question. Through omission of actual facts, the executive had purposely misled the employee.

Here's the kicker: the information the executive was hiding would not have been detrimental to the company to divulge. Rumors were already rampant about the upcoming change. Some meetings about changing the product line were openly communicated, so the momentum was obvious. The official announcement four weeks later (before there was a completed plan) was preceded by internal discussions. The truth that change was afoot would have harmed nothing.

Upon learning the facts, the employee, whose job was unaffected, moved to another company anyway because his trust in the executive and the company was erased by this five-second conversation that contained *a* truth but not *the* truth.

It is amazing that lies are almost always revealed over time. Transparency protects the leader from such scenarios.

★ ★

IMPLEMENTATION: *Establish a policy of transparency.*

I received a call one afternoon from a woman who had served as CEO of an organization for only a year. It did not take long for her to observe that the organization had "dead brain cells." In truth, the organization had become fossilized, frozen in its past and with no desire to move forward. The symptoms were everywhere. Decision making was restricted to the five division directors.

Inside the organization, inefficiencies ruled because people did not dare make even the smallest decision without permission from the appropriate division director. An $80,000 piece of equipment rested in a room for two years, waiting to be installed because no one uttered the words, "Install it." When a piece of equipment urgently needed to be replaced, no one could make the purchase because the division director was on a two-week vacation with orders that no one disturb him. It was common for all the decision makers to leave for extended periods of time without revealing how they might be reached. This effectively shut down each division for several weeks a year.

Each division director had risen through the ranks. Each had been with the organization for a minimum of twenty-five years; three had been there more than thirty years. The total of their professional experiences were accumulated in one place, so to say their worldview was narrow would be an understatement. The directors commonly responded to queries with, "This is the way we do it."

The new CEO wanted to implement changes at a place that had not changed in thirty years. She was met with immediate resistance. The directors ignored her orders. They did not complete projects and gave her a recurring list of excuses. One director actually told the CEO, "I have been here through six CEOs. I will be here after you are gone, too."

Indeed, he had been through six CEOs. But he did not outlast this one. Neither did the other four division directors—within six months they had all been removed. These removals did not meet with universal acclaim, as some people missed having no accountability. They missed not having to think. The significant culture shift unnerved those who remained.

The CEO set up principles of the organization, beginning with herself:

1. *The door to the CEO's office is open if you have opinions or concerns. Come in and talk.*
2. *The administration will operate with total transparency. You will know what decisions have been made that affect the total organization, and you will be given an explanation as to why these decisions were made.*
3. *E-mails that update what is happening within the organization will be sent to all employees on a regular basis.*
4. *Monthly staff meetings will be held and all employees are invited. The CEO will be present to answer your questions.*
5. *You are welcome to disagree with a decision, but you are expected to implement the decision to the best of your ability. Accountability is now a stated value of the company.*
6. *Day-to-day decisions should go through the appropriate chain of command.*
7. *Innovation is encouraged. Share your ideas. You can help us be better at what we do.*
8. *An innovation account will be set up to fund the ideas of employees.*
9. *We will value our company, its mission, and each other. To that end, employees will treat each other with courtesy, and offer personal support of corporate goals across all divisions.*
10. *We are all in this together. No one works on an island.*

The symbolism of these efforts is clear. There are no hidden agendas; in the words of the late comedian Flip Wilson, "What you see is what you get!" Those outside the decision-making process now had the opportunity to ask questions and give feedback. Indeed, participation in the process was encouraged.

The culture of the place began to shift as people recognized two significant changes: each person would have a voice if he chose to use it, and there would be no hidden agendas. Everything, *everything*, would be in the open.

The truth is that people do not have to agree with you to be a committed follower. They do need to understand you. These corporate values must become connected to our personal values. By connecting personal values to corporate values, we are able to overcome the self-interest that sometimes rules our decision making. Decisions based on self-interest most often lead to loss of credibility and reputation.

CORPORATE VALUES

A universally accepted system of corporate values not only protects the company from poor employee behavior and performance, it also protects the company's image with customers and vendors.

A clearly articulated set of corporate values, published and lived by, can change the behavior of employees due to their desire to conform to those values. In fact, says the research, employees who cannot live up to these values may quit.

Author and business consultant Jim Collins describes the process in *Good to Great*, saying, "Those people who do not share the company's core values find themselves surrounded by corporate antibodies and ejected like a virus."[7]

CEOs tell me that they do not want to lose "good employees" to a set of values. Why would you want employees who cannot live up to your values? Leaders are the people who carry forward the important corporate messages, and few messages are more important than corporate values. These values must be defined and repeated in order to align employees with values that can evolve a positive corporate culture. They also can be reinforced from any position, so a person occupying the lowest corporate positions, but having chosen leadership as a vocation, can play this role.

★ ★

IMPLEMENTATION: *Define your corporate values.*

Value systems can be worded in different ways, whether in short statements or whole paragraphs.
Here are three concepts that collectively create a basic system of corporate values:

> *We are customer focused. We believe it. We live it. A customer's problem is everybody's problem. The solution starts with me.*

> *We are colleague focused. We treat our colleagues with respect. We respond with integrity, candor, courtesy, and urgency.*

> *We are teamwork focused. My company is first. My unit is second. We all share in success and failure.*

I found this in my files but have no idea which of the many companies with which I have worked uses this. I wish I did because I'd love to give credit.

These corporate values are only examples, but they clearly foster values of collaboration and interdependence. Write your own and live by them. Let everyone see you live by them so the values will be implanted upon the culture of your organization. Scandals in business, politics, and in our personal lives mean a clearly articulated set of values is more important than ever if we truly want to do the right things the right way.

Jerome Kohlberg of the equity firm Kohlberg Kravis Roberts & Co. makes the case in this fashion: "All around us there is a break down in values . . . It is not just the overpowering greed that pervades our business life. It is in fact that we are not willing to sacrifice for the ethics and values we profess. For an ethic is not an ethic and a value not a value without some sacrifice to it."[8]

The reason we do not make the sacrifice is the absence of courage and humility, two traits essential to a good leader. In the absence of these traits, we promote personal self-interest above values, a condition that sometimes results in the corporate scandals with which we have become far too familiar. Any time self-interest is a prime motivator, we create a culture of moral ambiguity so that wrong is not easily definable and right is whatever results in short-term gratification.

One company uses a "covenant" that each employee signs. The covenant presents in clear form the values of the company, followed by a pledge by the employee to live these values on the job. The employee signs the pledge at the bottom of the page.

This approach has obvious advantages, largely because it relies less on leaders carrying the corporate value message and it removes any doubt as to whether these values are to be applied. An employee pledge that is part of a review is a powerful communication and motivation tool.

★ ★

THESE LEADERSHIP TRAITS ARE ESSENTIAL TO DEFINE WHAT WE EXPECT FROM THOSE WE LEAD AND TO SHOW OTHERS HOW WE CONDUCT BUSINESS. By operating with integrity, honesty, and humility, we not only share our expectations of employee attitudes and behavior, but also relieve ourselves of the unproductive task of constantly managing people who should have permission to perform their own jobs within the boundaries we have outlined. We and they will become more productive as a result. Courage, which allows us to do all of the above, becomes an expectation of ourselves and of others. Adopting these traits is a crucial step in becoming a White Hat leader.

CHAPTER FOUR

GIVE YOUR EMPLOYEES
WHAT THEY NEED

White Hat Principles:

★ *There is a main driver of employee performance, the "craving."*
★ *Personnel value gives employees a sense of relevance to the organization.*
★ *Pride in an organization generates commitment and loyalty from employees.*
★ *Permission to become a leader opens opportunities for dialogue.*

Employees respond to many factors including pay, benefits, and recognition, and managers usually use these items to "motivate" employees. However, these baseline items, although important, are the most superficial of answers in motivating employees. It is a leader's job to identify and initiate the *real* drivers of personal performance.

There is a main driver of employee performance, the "craving."

ONE EVENING I CAME HOME AND WALKED INTO A FAMILIAR SCENE WITH MY FAMILY.

"Where do you want to go for dinner?" my wife asked.

I did not hesitate. "I crave Mexican food tonight!"

"Mickey D's," came the response from my youngest son, Thomas.

"Ugh," said my oldest son, Reeves. "I'm craving pizza."

My wife delivered a fourth option. "How about dinner at a really nice restaurant?" she offered.

There we were, four people all equally in need of dinner, but with totally different cravings.

Just as people crave different foods at mealtime or crave different results from a relationship, people crave different things from work. These cravings are a desire to gain something additional from the work experience that makes employment more satisfying. We all want many other, smaller things as well, but in general people have a single driving force in their employment from which they get satisfaction. As you observe what drives your own employees to perform at their peak, you may discover even more cravings than the ones that appear here.

As I developed and tested my own theory of five cravings in the workplace, I also began to identify people who exhibit these cravings. Once I knew the main driver of personal performance, the craving, it became my job to initiate that drive in each individual. It works!

THE CRAVING TO CONQUER

Conquerors want your problems because they desire to overcome problems, barriers, or simple stagnation. These are your innovators, your "out of the box" thinkers who are happiest when on the attack. Keep them busy with resolving the issues that can move your organization in a forward direction and you both will be successful.

Somewhere in the mid-70s I identified that this is what makes me happiest on the job. My motivation is to seek challenges and the success of overcoming them. One of my former bosses called it "the solution mentality"—the need to see a challenge, identify a solution that does not yet exist in the system, and to initiate that solution from scratch.

You can easily identify the Crave to Conquer in the employee who readily volunteers to be a part of problem-solving teams. This individual will demonstrate creativity, throwing around ideas with almost reckless abandon. To some extent, the quality of the idea is not as relevant as the discussion it generates, which likely leads to another, better idea. This person adds energy and urgency to the discussion, challenging, cajoling, and ultimately collaborating with others in this earnest effort to overcome the challenge at hand.

Those who Crave to Conquer are usually not interested in leading implementation of the plan or managing the result of the implementation. Implementing and maintaining do not provide the same rush as creating solutions. The employee loses enthusiasm, focus, and energy. You can watch the balloon deflate as impatience and frustration take over. My own employment history is a prime example, as my résumé reflects my accepting jobs that require building something different than what I inherit. As the résumé will attest, I would accomplish the mission in about a year, struggle to stay energized for some months, then seek and accept a new job with new challenges. This was why I changed jobs every two years.

CONQUERORS WANT YOUR PROBLEMS BECAUSE THEY DESIRE TO OVERCOME PROBLEMS, BARRIERS, OR SIMPLE STAGNATION BY CREATING SOMETHING NEW.

I am faced with similar résumés when people apply for a job with me, and I inquire about the reason for this job hunting. The answer is often a mirror reflection of my own behavior. They will say, "It was fun when we were building a new department [or company, or campaign, whatever the scenario]. Once we finished I became bored." Sometimes, that is the perfect answer for the job I have available.

Maybe Conquerors are attention-deficit and need new challenges to stay focused. More than likely, they are people who need a high degree of stimulation to remain engaged over a long period of time. For whatever reason, Conquerors are strong personalities who crave a mission, and pity the poor person who gets in the way of success.

★ ★

IMPLEMENTATION: *Leading the Conqueror*

Leading this person requires a deft hand, as communication will sometimes be confrontational (although confrontation is usually issue-oriented rather than personal). The "in your face" language used by the Conqueror is intended to push that envelope to the limit and to insert the Conqueror's sense of urgency rather than to be judgmental or to cause conflict. Conquerors want decisions and action now! Delays or, worse, a change in a decision from above, will frustrate the Conqueror's desire to attack a problem, issue, or project. Although at times it may be difficult to discern, the communication style is much more about getting to the right solution than being arrogant. He has no time to deal with the minutiae so his language is used to remove the nitpicky from the equation in order to resolve the big issues as quickly as possible. This requires the leader to step back for an assessment of the motive before responding or face the consequence of sending the Conqueror into a blue funk that robs the leader of the positive traits at his disposal.

The leader should engage the Conqueror with questions that cause the Conqueror to defend his position. This Q&A approach allows for the laser-beam analysis on which the Conqueror thrives. The Conqueror will accept the questions as a challenge, likely delivering an on-point response. If questions do not present themselves to you, ask for further explanation by saying, "Educate me on how you reached that conclusion." Whether question or statement, you should use language that inquires.

Creating new challenges for the Conqueror that are consistent with his mission are welcome. If the finance department is having issues with his suggestions, make it his responsibility to justify outcomes in terms that will win over the "bean counters." He will happily take on all comers.

The Conqueror thrives on feedback, giving back in kind any arguments tossed his way. Keep the discussion going by allowing it to be one-sided a majority of the time so that he can think out loud and you can view his process. One of the excellent traits of a Conqueror is that he knows what he knows and knows what he does not know. His self-worth is based on successful completion of the building process, so he is hesitant to bluff in the event you, or anyone else, may possess information that can help him succeed. If you ask a direct question to which he does not know the answer, the Conqueror will admit his lack of knowledge and follow by asking you where he might find the answer.

★ ★

THE CRAVING TO CLIMB

The Climber is ambitious and is eager to learn all that can be learned about the company. He wants to know what is happening above him, below him, and on either side of the position he holds. The more he knows and the more he does, the more likely he will move upward and onward within the organization, which is his ultimate goal and therefore his craving.

As with the Conqueror, the Climber is easily identified because his core traits are clearly visible. This is the traditional way in which we view our employees, although this chapter proves that we cannot view everyone in the same light.

Ascending the corporate ladder is what motivates the Climber and this intent becomes so important that the leader cannot ignore the Climber without risking losing this employee. Dead-end positions thwart the Climber, so he will resign as soon as possible after perceiving there is no way to rise through the ranks.

THE CLIMBER IS AMBITIOUS AND IS EAGER TO LEARN ALL THAT CAN BE LEARNED ABOUT THE COMPANY. HE WANTS TO KNOW WHAT IS HAPPENING ABOVE HIM, BELOW HIM, AND ON EITHER SIDE OF THE POSITION HE HOLDS.

Salary matters to Climbers, but more for the status implied by the income. Money, to the Climber, is a way of keeping score.

Because the Climber craves leadership in order to prove a point—that he deserves higher status—you may catch your first glimpse when, for example, a Climber in finance enters your office to explain how marketing can do a better job. This betrays the Climber's tendency to insert himself in areas outside his own venue in order to demonstrate his command of the organization's big picture.

He will readily volunteer for any task force and committee to get a glimpse of what makes others successful. This also reveals his tendency to need association with people he perceives have power.

Climbers are often vocal in meetings as they attempt to prove their value with ideas, criticisms, and general comments about almost anything. Sometimes this results in too much communication as this frequent insertion of comments begins to dominate the dialogue within a meeting. Resentment by others can be a negative outcome of this tendency.

You will watch the Climber attempt to formulate and lead small groups so that he can accomplish two goals: (1) demonstrate leadership ability that gets results, and (2) become eligible to lead even larger groups that address more complex and important problems.

★ ★

IMPLEMENTATION: *Leading the Climber*

Climbers may appear selfish, but they are great employees when their focus is correctly channeled toward corporate goals and away from personal interests, although the Climber will continue to perform for his own benefit. Leaders should take advantage of this corporate zealot and do what great leaders often do: delegate. The very nature of the Climber requires that he succeed, so when given accountability, the Climber tends to give it his all to reach success.

Leading the Climber means allowing him to be self-sufficient and to lead without interference from the boss. Intervention from above diminishes his ability to demonstrate his worth. Frustration with the boss is the inevitable result.

The best way to communicate with a Climber is to assign him a specific task to be achieved by a specific time. There should be "check-in" times so the leader can stay informed of progress, but otherwise let the Climber go full bore—and he will.

You motivate Climbers by turning them loose, but with strict deadlines and regularly scheduled meetings that emphasize personal accountability. Many employees despise being held accountable, but these meetings reinforce to the Climber that his successes are being noticed. The Climber will never be happier, and you will likely receive great results.

★ ★

CRAVES A CAUSE

Cravers of a Cause believe in value systems that work for everybody. Fairness and consistency are traits they both admire and exhibit. Many people in service organizations crave a cause. After all, that is what brought them to the service area. They want to make a difference.

I occasionally offer my services to my religious denomination. A recurring issue is in persuading ministers to achieve administrative competencies such as accounting and personal management, a difficult task because pastors are not interested in these things. They have a cause that attracted them to the ministry. Not one of them entered the ministry in order to keep financial records or handle staff issues.

Many employees face this same plight. They crave a cause but find themselves in jobs that are task-centered rather than value-centered. The key is to help these individuals find a cause within their jobs. Money is not the prime motivator for Cravers of a Cause. The work is not as important as the *outcome* of the work, because they need validation that some greater good is being accomplished.

CRAVERS OF A CAUSE BELIEVE IN VALUE SYSTEMS THAT WORK FOR EVERYBODY. FAIRNESS AND CONSISTENCY ARE TRAITS THEY BOTH ADMIRE AND EXHIBIT.

Many HR administrators in companies possess this same service mentality. They believe their jobs *help* people, even though employees rarely perceive them in that light. One HR executive explained his job this way: "Many of my HR colleagues think their job is to put out fires. That's a negative view. I help people be happy at the company. I tell them the benefits of working here. I help them with their problems. It makes me feel good when I create positive outcomes for our employees. That's my role and my goal."

Excellent trainers approach training with the same fervor that an elementary school teacher approaches a class. They believe that what they do makes a difference. Their cause is to make each employee better at what they do, which helps the employee flourish in the organization and helps the organization achieve greater results. One trainer views her job this way: "I am a teacher and a mentor. And I am passionate about it!"

Even some executives, as hard-boiled as they are supposed to be, thrive in an environment where they can improve circumstances for employees, customers, and the company.

★ ★

IMPLEMENTATION: *Leading the Craver of a Cause*

Value outcomes are the prime motivator. For example, a marketing director of a bank was interested in supporting research for breast cancer, a disease that had taken her mother. The bank president suggested it would be possible for the bank to support an annual marathon to raise money for research. The marketing director ran with the idea, ultimately producing an annual event that raised thousands of dollars. The bank began to sponsor awareness meetings and screenings, and provided volunteers for direct mail campaigns. In a few years, the bank was awarded special recognition for its work in the field of breast cancer research. The bank's visibility in the community became extremely high because of the passion of the marketing director.

Of course, the marketing director continues to perform her other tasks as well, but at a higher level. Her job can become connected to her cause. She could not be happier. Neither could the bank.

★ ★

CRAVES A CRAFT

The employee who Craves a Craft wants to be exceptionally good at what she does. She has chosen this line of work because this is what excites and motivates her. She tends to identify herself with her job, and as a result, her worth is tied to how well she perceives she is doing her job.

Those in the Crave-a-Craft mode always want to know more and do better. These people constantly ask to attend seminars so they can learn more about their areas of employment. They desire to be cutting-edge employees in their work area.

THE EMPLOYEE WHO CRAVES A CRAFT WANTS TO BE EXCEPTIONALLY GOOD AT WHAT SHE DOES. SHE HAS CHOSEN THIS LINE OF WORK BECAUSE THIS IS WHAT EXCITES AND MOTIVATES HER.

Employees in information technology departments often fall into this category. Their passion for their work pushes them to know the newest, greatest development. This is equally true with people who provide financial services, especially those who work in retirement or investment areas.

Money is often less important to those who Crave a Craft than the opportunity to improve their job skills. I have seen people in IT ask that, instead of receiving a raise, the money be used to allow him or her to attend an additional technology conference. Promotions are less important, because the promotion inside their department may mean less time spent on the craft in order to assume management functions. For the Craves-a-Craft personality, knowledge and the freedom to apply it is the prime motivator.

★ ★

IMPLEMENTATION: *Leading the Craver of a Craft*

The key communication technique for these cravers is to acknowledge and honor their expertise. The best opening line you can provide is, "You are the expert on this," as this simple statement affirms the status she seeks. The worst thing you can do is fake knowledge of their craft. A simple "I don't know" will garner far more respect than an attempt to sound as if you know something that you don't. After all, their knowledge is what you pay them to provide. It is insulting to imply that you do not need them.

People who depend on their job for their self-identity often require an enormous amount of praise and affirmation. Although confident in their skills, these cravers need steady positive feedback from those whose opinions they value. They often take criticism of their work as a personal attack, making feedback a delicate task for the leader. Tread lightly and with carefully chosen words when you need to be critical.

When in need of correcting a Craft employee, begin the conversation with, "The first thing I want to do in this meeting is tell you that I recognize the enormous abilities you bring to this organization." This simple affirmation diffuses the criticism to come, although the criticism may still have a morale-deflating impact on the Craves-a-Craft employee.

★ ★

CRAVES A BALANCE

A Balancer views work as important but not as a prime motivator. Work must coexist with other facets of life.

Ironically, this craving most often occurs at extreme ends of a person's work life. The new generation of employees often desires a balance between work life and social life. These young people enjoy working alongside those with whom they would also like to share a drink or a meal. Extending their social life to the workplace makes work more fun.

These employees stay at companies longer when the people they work with are similar to them in terms of age and interests, including fashion, movies, and music. You can often receive a reality check as to the longevity you can expect from a young employee by observing whether or not they hang out with their coworkers at lunch, after work, and on weekends.

As we grow older and have families, we tend to want balance between family and work. Most of us with families attempt this balance at some time during our work lives. In truth, most of us are unsuccessful, usually choosing one over the other.

★ ★

IMPLEMENTATION: *Leading the Balancer*

The best motto for such people is this: family comes first. This means we must sometimes accept an employee's arriving late or leaving early to care for a sick child or an ailing parent. As a way of demonstrating my support, I have allowed employees to take a few hours away from work to tend to family matters without having to use vacation time or sick leave. Although this approach is likely controversial to those who desire a strict workplace, it has never failed to create a loyal employee who works extra hard to get the job done. Employee loyalty is a result I will gladly exchange for a couple of hours away.

Most organizations with a low turnover rate have adopted some flexibility to allow work and private lives to coexist, including short periods of time away without penalty, or "flex time," which allows employees to work nontraditional schedules.

When these employees are evaluated each year along with their colleagues, you can inject concerns about family leave, although the vast majority of employees are careful not to abuse this privilege. They know that flexibility, which is their major concern with the job, is not available from all employers. Flexibility is the prime motivator for enjoying their job and is more important than rewards and recognition.

Communicate your expectations to the person who craves balance. My own approach is to simply say, "I judge you on achieving results in a timely fashion. As long as you meet these expectations, you have the flexibility you need."

★ ★

IMPLEMENTATION: *What are the cravings of your staff?*

Try this revealing exercise. Ask each of your employees what will make him or her happy on the job. The employees will probably fail the first time because they will give you what they think you want to hear. Don't allow that shortfall. Ask again in a different way based upon the answers you receive. Since you're looking for their cravings, refine the inquiry until you receive an accurate picture of what drives each employee. Once you have identified the driving factors, you will be in a position to create loyalty and a culture that increases human productivity as well.

★ ★

Personnel value gives employees a sense of relevance to the organization.

IN ORDER TO RECOGNIZE, motivate, and truly lead an employee, there must be an understanding in clear terms of what that person contributes. A supervisor needs to understand value beyond simple tasks, and the employee will be more loyal when that value can be stated. Personnel value, then, is approached from MONEY AND POSITION DID NOT MAKE THE TOP TEN WHEN EMPLOYEES WERE ASKED ABOUT JOB SATISFACTION.

two ends of the relationship: the supervisor understanding the true value of the employee, and the employee hearing that his value is embraced.

Stating value to an employee is often done with incentives or rewards systems, which can be effective when consistently and fairly applied. If you use these systems, you know that they can also be fraught with problems.

As noted earlier, money and position did not make the top ten when employees were asked about job satisfaction. What did make the top ten, coming in at number four, is receiving recognition and praise for the work performed.[1] Personnel value gives employees a sense of relevance to the organization.

Only those within the organization whose integrity is sufficiently acknowledged can give messages of personal worth so that the value is truly received. Otherwise, the recognition is considered insincere, even manipulative.

Harvard researchers have written much about a concept called "Walk Around Management." In simple terms, WAM involves managers briefly visiting employees to acknowledge and to praise them. For example, a boss using WAM tours offices and tells one employee, "Good job, Bobby. We could not do this without you."

As the boss exits Bobby thinks to himself, "He doesn't know what the hell I do." And he's probably right. The "atta boy" statement has lost its luster because it does not connect the employee to an actual value. WAM is most effective when it goes beyond expressions of "good job." It becomes magical when you can tell the individual exactly how he or she is valuable.

Let's take an example of a secretary who has produced a report under deadline. The report evolves into a proposal, and the proposal evolves into a contract. The big wheels in the executive suite are slapping themselves on the back in celebration of a mighty corporate victory.

TALK LESS ABOUT THE WORK THAN ABOUT THE OUTCOME OF THE WORK. ARTICULATE TO THE EMPLOYEE THAT THE WORK RESULTS IN SOME HIGHER RESULT.

One of them walks to the secretary and says, "Melissa, you did a good job on that report. Thanks." And she says "thank you" and gets back to work.

Another executive walks up to her desk and says, "Melissa, I have been thinking. I remember when you worked so hard to meet the deadline on that report. If we hadn't made that deadline, none of the other events would have happened. You have as much to do with this big contract as anyone. I want you to know that I know you made this happen."

Melissa floats out of her chair because her value has been defined. Melissa did not just do a good job on the report. She made a difference, and that difference has been precisely defined.

Personnel value gives employees a sense of relevance to the organization and is a powerful ingredient for a healthy culture.

Talk less about the work than about the outcome of the work. Articulate to the employee that the work results in some higher result.

One morning before sunrise, the CEO of a theme park walked the park. He came upon a man repairing a ride.

"Will the ride be operational today?" the CEO inquired.

"Sure," replied the repairman. "It'll be running fine."

"That's great," said the CEO. "Our surveys say this is the favorite ride of our customers who are between three and five years old. They would be so disappointed if the ride was not working." He continued, "It must be great to know that your work brings such happiness to these children. Without you, today might be very sad day."

The workman's rather mundane task had been transformed into something greater than the work itself. The man's face moved from a tired frown to a wide grin. He realized that his work made a difference. His value had been stated.

> SPEAK IN TERMS OF OUTCOMES, SUCH AS GIVING PEOPLE BETTER FINANCIAL SECURITY, OR MAKING PEOPLE HAPPIER, MORE KNOWLEDGEABLE, OR SAFER.

Providing personnel value requires redefining work so it has greater meaning. Speak in terms of outcomes, such as giving people better financial security, or making people happier, more knowledgeable, or safer.

★ ★

IMPLEMENTATION: *Value your own staff.*

Write down the names of people with whom you work and next to each name, list the person's value—not her job, but her value. Your employees' value is the difference they make to you, a colleague, or the company. It may be something as small as "You get everything in on time and that keeps us all on time," or "I saw the way you handled that upset customer. We kept that customer because of you." These things add value to the everyday work of employees, and make the employees feel valued.

★ ★

*Pride in an organization generates commitment
and loyalty from employees.*

CEOS CAN LAUNCH AND BUILD PRIDE, although experience shows it is most effective when driven by leaders on the front line, the people who are closest to the work of the organization.

An article in the August 2003 issue of *Fast Company* defines pride-driven leaders as such: "These leaders believe that commitment and loyalty derive solely from the relationship that they strike with the people who report to them. So they personalize the workplace, cultivating close-knit communities inside larger, often impersonal corporations."[2]

★ ★

IMPLEMENTATION: *Build pride in your culture.*

Pride-building leadership on the front lines is a first cousin to Walk Around Management at the executive level. The major difference is the effort to create and court groups of people rather than individuals, and to extend business relationships to a personal level, although always keeping some distance so the leader may protect authority. This distance is acceptable because the pride-driven leader is creating "push" from the peer group to its individual members. The ultimate goal is to create better performance for the company, one cluster of employees at a time.

The fund-raising division of a foundation was facing just such a situation after its director resigned. The group, which had not had the benefit of good management or leadership, faced a withering economy that was resulting in nationwide declines in charity donation. Individual giving had declined for two successive years, and corporate giving was on a significant downward spiral. Morale was declining as well.

The new director knew that improving morale was the initial step to financial turnaround. Unless everyone worked at peak levels, all new efforts were doomed to fall short of their potential.

The first staff meeting set the tone. "I believe in you," were the first words the new director spoke to the staff. "You have been a first-class staff producing better than average results until two years ago. We need to go back to how we felt and operated when we were hitting on all cylinders."

That's fine, was the response. We used to think we were good, said the group, but we're feeling beaten up at the moment.

"Okay," replied the new director, "let's get control of our own destiny. What can we do to improve our fund-raising efforts while cutting back our expenses?"

The staff was stunned. No one had asked their opinion before so the question froze them. Fifteen seconds of silence followed, but the new director refused to fill the void. Within another five seconds came the torrent of ideas ranging from innovation to specific budget cuts.

A staff retreat was organized during which two days were spent sharing and sometimes arguing, both in the spirit of lifting everyone's performance. The group adopted a slogan: *We will do it!*

The annual goal was surpassed before the end of the second quarter. The all-time corporate fund-raising record was surpassed within the third quarter of the fiscal year.

This staff had never received bonuses based upon performance so no financial reward was anticipated. Their achievement was the result of having pride in themselves and their colleagues, the peer pressure to perform at the highest levels every single day. It was only when these employees made success a personal issue, rather than a foundation issue, that they reached full potential.

Jon Katzenbach, in his book *Why Pride Matters More Than Money*, outlines basic elements of creating a pride-driven culture.

1. *Personalize the workplace.* Katzenbach claims leadership commitment is the single best way to build the requisite bond with employees. Personal commitment from the leadership requires a personal relationship with the employees. For example, a department director called his ill employees daily to check on their status. He offered professional psychological support for a woman who lost her baby and for a man who was robbed. Flowers and food were sent to homes. The support system that the director established brought the staff together.

2. *Set your focus on pride rather than financial reward.* "The journey is more important than the destination," writes Katzenbach. Pride is about what people do everyday rather than about reaching goals. Those goals are reached, but it is only by quality work

performed one day at a time. This is why it is important to stop and celebrate benchmarks of success so that everyone enjoys the journey.

3. *Localize whenever possible.* This is the idea of creating small group communities that share a common purpose. As Katzenbach says, what works in one setting may not work in another. The more localized and defined the group, the better the results.

4. *Use simple messages.* Complexity is an evil intervener in the process of pride building. Stories about each other are particularly effective.[3]

John A. Byrne, editor in chief of *Fast Company*, sums it up by saying, "Work is indeed personal, as it always has been."[4]

★　★

Permission to become a leader opens opportunities for dialogue.

MANY PEOPLE in management positions believe they must lead by controlling the information, providing the brainpower, making the decisions, and directing the actions of others. This is what makes them managers rather than leaders.

White Hat leaders understand that those they lead have good minds and usually good intentions. They leverage the abilities of their people to gather even more information. They encourage people to ask questions and they offer ideas that will help everyone work from the same vision and will help them be engaged in making the office/company

MANY PEOPLE IN MANAGEMENT POSITIONS BELIEVE THEY MUST LEAD BY CONTROLLING THE INFORMATION, PROVIDING THE BRAINPOWER, MAKING THE DECISIONS, AND DIRECTING THE ACTIONS OF OTHERS. THIS IS WHAT MAKES THEM MANAGERS RATHER THAN LEADERS.

work at a higher level of proficiency. This is permission to make leadership a vocation, just as you were asked to give permission to yourself in the first chapter.

People function at a higher level when they are a part of the business decision-making process, and as a result leaders get better results for the company. A CEO of a company in the financial services industry told me a story about permission giving. The company was in need of "reengineering," one of those business terms that means the company needs a new vision and new organization in order to stay competitive. The process is gut-wrenching because every person in the organization has a stake in the outcome. For this reason, the CEO expected to receive total and wholehearted engagement from every person, particularly the executive team. Instead, the meetings of senior management seemed to end with the same question. "What do you want us to do?" they would ask.

"I want you to think!" he'd respond with great authority. But the next meeting would end with the same question as before: "What do you want us to do?"

One night at dinner, he expressed his frustration to his wife who asked a question: "Do they know it's all right for them to offer you suggestions?" She added a zinger: "It sounds as if they are afraid to say anything."

This is when the CEO experienced his epiphany.

"I guess I come across as

PEOPLE FUNCTION AT A HIGHER LEVEL WHEN THEY ARE A PART OF THE BUSINESS DECISION-MAKING PROCESS

something of a bully, and I am certainly strong with my personal opinions. It dawned on me that over the years I had withdrawn my permission for them to feel free to offer suggestions. They had been trained to do what I told them to do rather than think for themselves. Now when I needed them most they were refusing to engage in the process. Believe me, the next meeting I began with assurances that I wanted their ideas and I was ready to listen. It took a while for them to believe me, but eventually we began working together. Even now, three years after we finished reengineering, I continue to tell them that they have permission to think and oftentimes act without worrying about me. That may be the best thing that came out of the process."

All of us are impacted by the way "authority figures" have given or withheld permission.

A friend of mine tells the story about the death of his grandfather. The death was not unexpected, so it was no surprise when the doctor summoned the family into a side room to give them the news.

The doctor began by explaining the hospital's effort to save the grandfather's life. As he went on, my friend's grandmother, in a state of denial, interrupted: "I don't understand. What are you saying?"

The doctor, a bit jolted from his narrative, replied, "Oh, I'm sorry. He passed away."

Hearing the news so directly, my friend's father began to weep. His mother wrapped her arms around him and said, "It's okay to grieve."

"No! It's not allowed," he said.

My friend responded to his father's reaction, saying, "Suddenly a door was opened up to my understanding of my father and why he was such an emotionally reserved man, even at age fifty-five. He had been raised in an environment in which his father had not given permission to express even basic human emotion. The result was that his now-deceased father's voice came to him from a childhood years ago telling him that men don't cry, and if you want to be a man you'd better dry those tears, mister."

★ ★

IMPLEMENTATION: *Grant employees permission to lead, and with that, permission to fail.*

All of us have questions about the boundaries of our behavior, in business and, as demonstrated above, in life. Giving or not giving permission is an amazing shaper of behavior. Its impact can be startling, even overwhelming.

Permission means we are allowed to think, to act, to explore, and to face the consequences of it all. Permission to become a leader opens opportunities for dialogue that cannot otherwise exist.

Consequences are a part of the equation—permission does not always mean we succeed, and giving permission does not mean that we work with immunity for the consequences of our actions. Permission to act includes permission to fail. This does not offer an excuse for failing, as failure carries with it the inherent consequences. However, employees will not risk sharing their thoughts or undergoing tenuous projects without some assurance that failure alone will not bring about reprimand. Mistakes are the natural by-product of trying to do anything exceptional, so they are to be expected from every employee who is trying to accomplish something positive on behalf of the company. For the effort alone they deserve some recognition, even if it is a sigh and, "Well, you were trying to do something good."

That statement begins the analysis of how to handle permission giving gone wrong. The first thing to look for is motive, meaning the reason why the employee undertook the act. A company-centered motive leaves much room for forgiveness of what went wrong. Second, did the employee directly cause the failure or did other factors derail the attempt? Third, were there obvious merits to the undertaking that deserve reward even in the face of failure?

The best course is usually to forgive mistakes of commission versus omission. The employee was trying to help. As one Microsoft VP observed, "I hate to fire someone for making a mistake. Look at all the valuable experience I would lose."

One of my sons once came to me concerned about trying out for the lead role in a school play. He said he was worried that he might not get the role. As I counseled him about the positive nature of trying, giving it your best shot, and other such platitudes, I realized that none of these things soothed his anxiety.

For some unknown reason I was struck by the memory of my grandmother chastising me when I was in elementary school. The teacher had asked that I sing a solo in a small class play and I had refused. My grandmother asked why I would not sing. I told her I was afraid I would be embarrassed. She shot me a look with her gray eyes.

"If you ain't failing, son, then you ain't trying," she barked.

"Are you afraid you'll be embarrassed?" I asked my son. He nodded.

"You have my permission to audition for the play and not get a single part in it," I said. "Furthermore, you have my permission to make a complete fool out of yourself." He giggled. "In fact, you have my permission to bring total shame upon the family!" He laughed out loud. "Son, if you ain't failing, you ain't trying!" We laughed together.

It turns out that, coincidentally, the lead role terrified him because it required singing. He was great, by the way.

In families and in the workplace few things motivate others to accomplishment more than permission giving. Permission to fail is a powerful motivator for success. It removes all judgment about whether or not we are worthy of respect or, more importantly, love. As leaders understand and embrace the concept that leadership is their vocation, so they also give permission to those with whom they work to accept leadership as a vocation. By granting this permission, leaders encourage free thinking and dialogue. This in turn generates ideas that can positively impact the workplace on professional and personal levels.

Ask yourself this question: are you capable of giving permission to your employees to become leaders and active participants in your work life? If not, you either have trouble delegating to people or you do not trust your people to have ideas and competencies beyond the tasks they perform. The first issue is yours to handle (with the help of this book).

The second issue is far more troublesome. For if you do not have faith in your people, you have surrounded yourself with poor employees. That is a situation that you must rectify before you place yourself in harm's way.

S UCCESS IS ALWAYS DEPENDENT UPON HAVING THE RIGHT PEOPLE IN THE RIGHT POSITIONS, working at high speed while performing the right tasks at the right time. The next chapter outlines how to make it happen.

CHAPTER FIVE

GATHERING THE TEAM

White Hat Principles:

- ★ *Understand the state of your organization and hire people that "fit" versus hiring people for skills.*
- ★ *Something should always be changing. If nothing is changing, you face stagnation.*
- ★ *Bad hire, quick fire.*
- ★ *Companies should invest time and money into training.*
- ★ *The ability to perform tasks well does not qualify an employee to assume a leadership position.*

L EADERS RELY ON THEIR TEAMS TO CREATE GOOD RESULTS. Teams are composed of individuals, of course, so it is necessary to create a unit that can work together. Skills can be taught, but chemistry must be created. That's the concept behind the first principle of this chapter. Principle number two recognizes that people and teams become stagnant when the organization becomes stagnant. White Hat leaders constantly create new ways to keep the energy level high. The third principle is a slogan I will one day place on a T-shirt: Bad hire, quick fire. We live too long with our mistakes, which is itself a mistake. The next principle is supported by a lot of research: very few investments bring a greater return than training. Even so, many in leadership positions loathe spending money on educating their employees, an error that costs much more money than can possibly be saved. The final principle warns of the difference between tasking skills and leadership skills that often results in a former superior employee becoming an inferior employee when promoted.

Understand the state of your organization and hire people that "fit" versus hiring people for skills.

MOST OF THE APPLICANT POOL WILL HAVE MOST OF THE BASIC SKILLS WE SEEK. Not all, mind you, but most. And depending upon the position (frontline employee versus upper-tier management), most of the personnel we bring on board will need some degree of training.

For the frontline employee, the training may be substantial since the employee may not have a lot of job experience doing much of anything. For a middle or senior management position, you are looking for specific skills and experiences. Those necessary skills readily appear on the résumé and during any subsequent interview. Even so, upon hiring, you will want to upgrade this person's skills to meet your key and specific requirements

ALTHOUGH RESEARCH IS TO THE CONTRARY, SOME SENIOR LEVEL MANAGERS CONTINUE TO PUT FORTH THE CONCEPT THAT VALUES, COMMUNICATION, AND CULTURE SKILLS ARE "SOFT."

even when promoting from within. If you do not, you are allowing a possible competency gap to exist that will be exposed only when a mistake is made. That is too late.

Although research is to the contrary, some senior level managers continue to put forth the concept that values, communication, and culture skills are "soft." As noted in the introduction, these are hard skills because they lead to hard numbers, such as productivity, return on investment, and profit. The improvement of these numbers should be a goal for anyone in an executive position. Given that a higher level of human productivity is attained when a manager/leader understands the principles already presented in this book, it seems preposterous that anyone would diminish their importance. Here are core principles of hiring that go beyond hard skills assessment.

HIRE PEOPLE WHO GO TOGETHER

Diversity of background and experience is imperative to business success. They "go together" when they operate from the same core as the organization.

One CEO tells me that his prime tactic for ensuring a healthy culture is hiring people who fit in, meaning their backgrounds are similar. This, he says, offers the greatest opportunity for finding commonality. In reality, this approach results in the total absence of diversity in the work force. If everyone has the same level of education, the same background, the same skills, and similar traits, the result is likely a narrow point of view.

If the employees have the same skills and background, they probably think the same. This approach to hiring parallels the idea of truth being incompatible with harmony. When everyone thinks the same way, there will be no dissension. This leads to a stress-free work life but a less than productive workplace. The differences we bring stir creativity through dialogue, even disagreement. These differences also serve to encourage discussions that test ideas, either showing their weaknesses or making them better.

The concept of "fitting in" restricts opportunities to succeed rather than enhancing them to the point that the business has become a social club rather than a business entity. The better approach is hiring people who *fit together* via their character, value systems, and universal acceptance of the corporate mission and vision. These are the points of commonality that matter, rather than that they all get along. Professionals with their eye on the corporate prize, however that prize is defined, will work together while also bringing their various views to the discussion, thereby forming a superior team. The concept of fitting together works when the emphasis is on the quality of people rather than an arbitrary demographic approach.

> THE CONCEPT OF "FITTING IN" RESTRICTS OPPORTUNITIES TO SUCCEED RATHER THAN ENHANCING THEM. . . . THE BETTER APPROACH IS HIRING PEOPLE WHO *FIT TOGETHER* VIA THEIR CHARACTER, VALUE SYSTEM, AND UNIVERSAL ACCEPTANCE OF THE CORPORATE MISSION AND VISION.

IMPLEMENTATION: *Look for chemistry.*

One executive director of a nonprofit uses the unique approach of having the staff identify chemistry with a potential new employee. The executive conducts the initial screening of résumés, chooses the people who are to be interviewed, and selects the finalists for the position. At the point when he is comfortable with either of the final two (no more than three) candidates, he invites separately each finalist to a catered lunch with staff. The executive does not participate in this lunch except to make introductions, remind staff of the role of the position within the office, and to advise that this gathering should be fun. By establishing a goal of social interaction rather than an opportunity to aggressively question the applicant's qualifications (that's the executive's role!), he offers a setting to discover if the "chemistry" exists between staff and applicant. The lunch is set for one hour but is allowed to go a bit longer if interaction is particularly positive. Following the final lunch, the executive calls in the staff for a discussion of perceptions about the applicants which concludes with the definitive question, "Who do *you* recommend?" The involvement of staff in this process is not a foolproof way to guarantee "fit," but it greatly improves the odds.

HIRE FOR CHARACTER

WE BEGIN THIS SECTION WITH AN OBSERVATION THAT IS LIKELY AFFIRMED BY YOUR OWN EXPERIENCES: people of good character make great employees, while people of bad character do not. Anyone who has worked with or supervised an employee who puts self above office, team, and organization can attest to the negative impact that behavior had on others. This is one of the reasons values receive such high priority in this book.

Your organization should ask questions at the applicant's place of employment. If the applicant would rather his current employer not know about the interview, move on to the next applicant. Even when the applicant has a legitimate reason for keeping intentions close to the vest, the fact that you cannot gain at least a cursory view of how that person operates in an office setting with colleagues robs you of valuable data that should be part of the decision-making process. You can ask for a personal reference, but the applicant may simply refer you to the only friend he has left.

On the application, request information that is not just job related. For example, volunteer and service activities within the community are a good sign of character and commitment to a value system. The absence of these may be a negative indicator or simply an omission, so inquire about such activities if they are indeed absent.

> PEOPLE OF GOOD CHARACTER MAKE GREAT EMPLOYEES, WHILE PEOPLE OF BAD CHARACTER DO NOT.

During the interview, create scenarios of conflict and ask how the applicant may resolve these conflicts. The answer may be different from the truth, as all applicants are on their best behavior, but the thought process revealed can be priceless.

Be sure the applicant meets with most of the staff that he or she will work with. The more the applicant talks to others, the more that is revealed about cultural and racial bias, conflict resolution techniques, and dialogue skills. Staff has a keen intuition about such things and will let you know if they see red flags. Certainly, some of the red flags may expose staff bias, which is not a bad thing to be aware of, either.

Be creative and come up with more ways to determine the nature of the applicant's character. This is important. Finding the hard skills is easy. Finding the soft skills is difficult.

★ ★

IMPLEMENTATION: *Apply tests of character.*

Chuck Pappalardo, managing director of Trilogy Venture Search, a recruiting firm in California, offers these tests of character to use when hiring new employees:

1. *Conduct an internal audit to assess your company's existing values.* Does it allow and encourage people to do the right thing? Is character discussed among top management? The purpose is to determine how a person of character might fit in.

2. *Profile the behaviors that your organization associates with character.* These fall under three categories: integrity, inspiring others, and humility. Develop interview questions that explore these behaviors.

   a. *Integrity*—Probe with questions such as, "Tell me about a time you faced a grave financial dilemma or difficult personal situation." The question should be open-ended to force the candidate to say more than a sentence.

   b. *Ability to inspire*—How does the candidate deal with bad news? Can the candidate be a consensus builder? The lead-in might be something like, "Tell me about a time you created a process or method to achieve a new result." Or ask about the last team built by the candidate. What worked and did not work?

   c. *Humility*—Listen for unsubstantiated claims of success. Ask self-awareness questions such as, "What is the biggest misperception people have of you?"[1]

★ ★

DO YOU NEED MAPPERS OR EXPLORERS?

PERSONALITY STYLES MAY DICTATE WHO YOU HIRE at a specific time in the corporation's evolution, because as companies change, so do their human resource needs. When CEOs ask about the type of people they need on staff, the answer, as it is so often, is that it depends on what you want to accomplish.

Some companies enter a maintenance period during which controlled growth is more important than rapid growth. This normally occurs when perfecting systems and/or products already in place is more important than changing systems and/or products.

EXPLORERS HAVE A STRONG SENSE OF CURIOSITY. THEY TEND TO ASK, "WHAT IF WE WENT THIS WAY INSTEAD?"

When an organization is in the maintenance mode, it needs people we will call "Mappers." Mappers are employees who follow instructions, or more precisely, the plan or "map" that has been presented to them. They do not deviate from that map. To use a technology phrase, they "plug and play."

Maintenance is what Mappers do best. Give an order and they follow it. They will not give you innovation or push the envelope with a thousand small ideas.

They "just do it." This is the type of person a leader needs when the organization wants to beat a rhythmic drum so that everyone stays in time with each other. You can squeeze out efficient use of resources, capital, and people with Mappers.

When an organization is entering a time of change, especially rapid change, a leader needs "Explorers." Explorers are always scanning the horizon for unfound territory, pushing ideas to management that will make the organization more creative and adaptable.

Explorers implant an entrepreneurial spirit on the organization because ideas breed innovation, and innovation breeds energy. Explorers have a strong sense of curiosity. They tend to ask, "What if we went this way instead?" or, "What might happen if we do this differently?"

Mappers and Explorers exist in all phases of life, personal as well as business. Most people tend to be one or the other, so a leader needs to have at least a sampling of each on staff in case the ship suddenly needs to change course. You can look at your team today and deduce which members fall into either category. They tell you by the way they act on the job and interact with you.

EXPLORERS ARE ALWAYS SCANNING THE HORIZON FOR UNFOUND TERRITORY, PUSHING IDEAS TO MANAGEMENT THAT WILL MAKE THE ORGANIZATION MORE CREATIVE AND ADAPTABLE.

Let me reduce this to a lowest common denominator with which many people identify. I am an Explorer. My wife is a Mapper. It is easy to identify us. When we go on vacation, my wife buys a map of the local area and plans our itinerary. We will go here and see that, then over here so we can see this, and the trip will be very organized.

I like to wander around, going no place in particular and wishing to see nothing specific. My attitude is, surprise me!

I recently traveled to Paris to give a speech, and my wife joined me on the trip. One night at about 10:00 p.m., craving a Parisian experience, I suggested we visit a sidewalk café that served crepes. She agreed.

As we exited the elevator in the lobby, I turned to head for the door. My wife made a turn in the opposite direction toward the concierge.

"Can you recommend a café?" she asked. "*Oui*," he replied.

"Do you have an address?" she asked. "*Oui*," was the response.

"Do you have a map?" Once again the answer was *oui* and the map was handed to her from across the desk.

Leaving the hotel, she unfolded the map and began looking for the address, which did not appear on the map. We walked until we reached an intersection.

"It's this way," she said, pointing to the left. This did not fit the directions I remembered receiving, but I dutifully followed her as she turned briskly to the left and walked with purpose. As we continued down the ever darker street, I remarked that the numbers on the buildings seemed to be going the wrong way given the address we were provided. She stopped and pointed to the map.

"Look at the map," she said. "This is the direction we must go." She seemed absolutely positive about her response, so I gulped before inquiring as to why we necessarily had to go in this direction.

"This is the only direction this street takes," she said in a rising tone. "It must be this way."

Not so, I noted. We could have turned right at the intersection rather than left. She insisted that the street did not go to the right.

"Yes it does," I said.

"No it does not," she responded, her voice now impatient with my perceived ignorance. "Look at the map!"

I looked, and sure enough, the map did not indicate that the street continued to the right at the intersection in question.

"The map is wrong," I declared, my voice now growing louder because I possessed knowledge she did not. "I looked to the right at that intersection and there is a street there."

"No there isn't! Look at the map!"

"Who are you going to believe," I demanded, "your husband, or a map made by the French?"

"I'll believe the map," she snapped.

We entered the Zone of No Return, a condition which does not allow either side of an argument to retreat or to give quarter of any kind. It was now all or nothing: one side had to be completely right and the other side completely wrong.

MAPPERS MUST HAVE A PLAN TO FOLLOW. THEY DO NOT LIKE TO LEAVE THE COMFORT OF KNOWING EXACTLY WHERE THEY ARE GOING.

It was now 10:20 p.m. in the City of Love and my wife and I were yelling at each other, veins bulging from our respective necks. The "he said/she said" phenomena of spousal argumentation was in full earshot for Parisians and tourists within a three-block area. Finally, she adopted an exit strategy. "Fine, I'm going this way," she screamed while pointing to her left, "and you can go anywhere you please." She walked into the darkness.

There I was, alone, watching my wife disappear. All the concerns of a husband came to mind. She could be mugged or even killed. What should I do? I went to the creperie, which was right where I thought it would be. She arrived a half an hour later, sat, ordered, and never mentioned that the map was wrong.

Mappers must have a plan to follow. They do not like to leave the comfort of knowing exactly where they are going. My wife believed the map even when the numbers on the buildings indicated the map was leading us away from our destination. This is not unlike a Mapper in a corporation who follows the strategic plan even when data shows the adopted strategy is not working. The Mapper ignores the bad numbers because he is attuned to follow a preconceived path to a predetermined goal.

GROWTH REQUIRES EXPLORATION AND INNOVATION. STABILITY REQUIRES BUILDING AND MAINTAINING THE PROCESSES THAT DELIVER PROFITABILITY.

As an Explorer, I was paying no special attention to my wife or the map during much of the journey from the hotel, choosing instead to take in the wonders of the Parisian night. I would have never asked the concierge for a map; instead, I would have wandered around until I stumbled upon an appropriate location. My way is not as direct, but it is, to me, a lot more fun. It also gives me options that I can choose to pursue. For example, if another street looks promising, I will deviate from my path and investigate the possibilities of this new course. Of course, my way might have resulted in our becoming lost, a condition that happens far more often than I wish to admit. The point is, Mappers tend to want a direct route and will not deviate from it. Explorers will use the map as a suggestion, if they use if at all. There are times in a company's life when one or the other personality trait is superior for what the company needs. Each has a place. Explorers are the ones who made the map and highlighted all the possibilities in the previously uncharted landscape. Mappers follow the map to build the roads and bridges that make the landscape habitable. One comes before the other.

Growth requires exploration and innovation. Stability requires building and maintaining the processes that deliver profitability. Companies that attempt fast growth when employing Mappers will find that growth is dependent upon doing things a different way and will fail. Companies that want to slow down to have time to build and maintain processes—while holding on to the Explorers who created the growth that outstretched the company's ability to deal with it—will discover that Explorers plus a mundane process equal disorganization. And neither style is intrinsically superior to the other. Each style has a role, depending on what you need from your company. Each can be effective when used correctly and each can be harmful when used incorrectly.

★ ★

IMPLEMENTATION: *Assess your direction.*

Step back and assess where you want your organization (office or team) to be within the year or two. Are you planning to implement change or slow down from a healthy pace? Remove or appropriately reassign the Mappers when you need Explorers, and vice versa.

It will take courage to do this, but it must be done. One of the secrets to success for a leader is having the right type of people to fulfill the vision. Do you have the right people? You need to answer this question before you even articulate the vision, because without the right people to implement it, the vision is doomed. Not only do you need the right people, you also need to have them in the right places.

★ ★

Something should always be changing. If nothing is changing, you face stagnation.

"IF IT AIN'T BROKE, DON'T FIX IT" is poor leadership strategy because leaders are constantly attempting to improve motivation, loyalty, and productivity through improving the chemistry of the office culture. One of the most effective techniques is through the introduction of new people to invade negative cultures with positive people. This takes time, of course, but from this point forward, consider that every new hire is an opportunity to improve culture. Likewise, a bad hire can hurt a positive culture, so there is an additional reason to pay closer attention to what an employee brings to the company beyond a set of skills.

Sometimes leaders inherit teams that were not of their choosing. It is usually too much to ask that the predecessor did a great job of hiring. This makes for a difficult situation for the new leader if she has a vision to cast. The casting cannot be accomplished until the personnel issues are resolved.

★ ★

IMPLEMENTATION: *Determine who you need on staff to implement the vision.*

Ask and answer these core questions before you determine the vision: Do you have the right positions? Do you have the right people in the right positions? Does the staff have relevant competencies that allow for reaching the goal? Where are the tensions between your office culture and the corporate culture? Where are the tensions between you and staff? Where are the tensions between and among staff members? Are there relationships that should be redefined? Are there relationships that should be initiated? Are there relationships that should be improved? Are there relationships that should be terminated?

Of course, a leader who has been in position for some years should be asking the same questions because leaders should always be testing the validity of the organization against the power of the vision. It is an ongoing and necessary process.

The guiding principle is that a stagnant employee pool makes for a stagnant organization. None of us wants high turnover rates among our employees, but a controllable rate of turnover is often very good for organizations that want to be high speed in their respective industries. Leaders understand that new blood usually brings different, valuable perspectives that allow an industrious leader to remold the organization into something better than existed before.

★ ★

Bad hire, quick fire.

I RECALL A STORY ABOUT A COMPANY THAT HIRED A MIDDLE LEVEL MANAGER WHO WAS GREAT—ON PAPER. The résumé was fantastic and the interview was better. This woman had it all. Experienced, ambitious, and smart as you can imagine, she blew away the other applicants to the point that there was no discussion about the qualifications of other applicants. She was a keen negotiator as well and had the hiring committee falling all over itself to make the deal.

Two weeks into her employment, a steady stream of complaining employees began its journey to the Personnel Department. She went on a business trip and took a couple of extra days at a spa without prorating the charges to the department, said one. She charged her personal mileage to the company, reported another.

A possible mistake, said the accountants. We'll issue a warning. And they did.

She cursed at one of the staff, a woman who was twenty minutes late because of a sick child and who had called in to let everyone know her situation. An HR violation, said the HR managers. We'll issue a warning. And they did.

The complaints kept coming. Employees reported temper tantrums, some as serious as one person saying she threw a letter opener at an employee who was too terrified to report the incident.

She waited until Thursday morning to announce a staff retreat that would take place on the following Saturday, leaving her employees in a turmoil as they attempted to juggle weekend responsibilities. Poor organizational skills, said one of the senior managers, but nothing so terrible that we should act.

WHEN YOU HIRE THE WRONG PERSON, ADMIT IT AS QUICKLY AS POSSIBLE. HANGING ON TO A BAD HIRE CREATES PROBLEMS THAT ARE NOT WORTH A DELAY IN FIRING.

When she entered the retreat setting she was wearing a T-shirt that stated, "I am a bitch and proud of it!" This was not meant to be cute. It was a personal value statement that revealed her leadership style.

The company's HR manager called her counterpart at the new employee's former company to have an unofficial, offline, we-never-had-this conversation between friends.

"Oh yeah," said the manager. "She has a terrible temper. We think she's dangerous. When she left here, her former employees danced down the hall singing 'Ding! Dong! The witch is dead.'"

The company tried what it called "rehabilitation." They attempted training sessions, anger management, and other intervention techniques. This person stayed with the company for almost eighteen months, inflicting pain wherever she went. Turnover in her unit, and even in units in close physical proximity to hers, skyrocketed. She never took responsibility or even feigned to understand why people would be upset with her. She threatened lawsuits, which, it turns out, was a ploy she used at her previous job.

Intervention techniques are not to be criticized. This woman's negative character, however, had been fully developed and was now largely unchangeable. She should have been fired long before the deed was done.

Why live with your mistakes? Resolve them. When you hire the wrong person, admit it as quickly as possible. Hanging on to a bad hire creates problems that are not worth a delay in firing.

For every day an unqualified, unhealthy, or disruptive person stays on the job, that person harms the company and is harmed himself. Allowing him to fail over and over prevents him from finding a place where he is better suited to work. And when the manager, probably surrounded by HR reps and lawyers, fires this person and states the reasons, the manager should also suggest some helpful criticism and ways to improve or find another position.

Companies should invest time and money into training.

ONCE HIRED, we should thoroughly train our employees in their positions as well as inform them as to what happens above and below the position. Giving employees this information is a set-up to training.

Employees are usually connected to other parts of their organizations, above and below as well as side-to-side. Paper flows from one area to the next, activities overlap, and people interact. The employee is not in isolation.

Companies should spend a lot of time and money on training due to the benefits they derive, not the least of which is a huge return on investment (ROI), as noted by numerous studies from a stockpile of universities.

COMPANIES SHOULD SPEND A LOT OF TIME AND MONEY ON TRAINING DUE TO THE BENEFITS THEY DERIVE, NOT THE LEAST OF WHICH IS A HUGE RETURN ON INVESTMENT.

Many organizations believe they do a good job of training and believe that they do a lot of training, even more than is required for excellent job performance. In truth, most do a poor job of training and not enough of it. Training is often an obligatory task that breeds no excitement and provides no energy. Trainers usually perform a stand-up lecture in a Ben Stein monotone, and trainees are rarely able to connect the dots.

The poster child for training is MSN.com, the upstart competitor to AOL and others. These employees are constantly in training. The result is that they are always confident that they know the latest information about any technology that affects their job performance. The employees are always motivated, focused, and driven to excellence. The opportunity to lose enthusiasm or to develop self-doubt is never present.

Any leader would never doubt the value of intense and ongoing training if exposed to one of the MSN.com sessions. Every session has a "wow" factor that motivates even mere observers.

These employees receive a variety of training approaches, including elaborate retreats, lectures, personal development projects, experiential learning models, interactive CDs, and feedback from management.

The diversity of training offered by MSN.com is a lesson for every organization on the planet.

Too many organizations use command-and-control training that I call Simple Task Operation (STO), the step-by-step process of starting and completing tasks without considering how they fit into the larger picture, or considering how an employee might be trained to respond to the process when an error occurs.

TEACHING THE FLOW OF WORK

Recall the importance of each person understanding her relationship with other areas of the office, including how her job performance impacts the ability of others to perform their jobs. This basic understanding of how her cog in the wheel is necessary in order for the wheel to roll provides a higher sense of personal value to the office and organization, which, in turn, generates a sense of urgency, connectedness to the organization as a whole as well as to its parts, and buy-in to the overall vision of the company.

GREAT TRAINING PROVIDES THE WHOLE PICTURE OF THE ORGANIZATION BY CONNECTING EMPLOYEES TO THE FLOW.

This reality is ignored when most organizations tend to focus only on highly specific mechanical training—training that relates to the job itself. My argument is this: every employee will operate at a higher level of efficiency when she understands the connection between her work and the rest of the company.

Here is an example. A manager trains that a form must be completed in such-and-such manner to be correct, and then the form should be passed on. The manager does not inform the employee of the next steps. What happens when that paper leaves the employee's office and flows into another's office? If the new employee does a good job, what impact does that have on the next step? What are the negative consequences if the form is handled incorrectly and passed on to the next level? Equally important is knowing who produced the form and why. What happened before the form reached the employee's office and what is the significance of this to the organization and the workflow process? And why is the employee not being told these things?

Many things move from one isolated area of the organization to another without anyone understanding the workflow or how one person's work affects the levels above, below, and to the sides of that person. Great training provides the whole picture of the organization by connecting employees to the flow, which has profound impact on efficiency in terms of both speed and accuracy.

Broadening the scope of training takes the employee from a small-screen-TV view to a wide-screen theater view with surround sound where it is easier to see and hear the large and small realities of the organization's workflow and the employee's connection to it. This is vital if we wish to help the employee better understand both the organization and the employee's place (and worth) within it.

DIVERSITY IN TYPE OF TRAINING

Diversity in type of training is a huge factor in creating an effective training program. Study after study of adult learning emphasizes that each person learns at a different pace and in a different way than the person sitting in the next chair.

The most common method of training is the lecture, involving one person delivering the information, often accompanied by PowerPoint slides or a flip chart. This is the least effective method of training. Studies show that this "stand and deliver" method results in low participant comprehension and a low level of retention.

In essence, lecturing is a data dump. There is so much data within these lectures that a person rarely can recall even sixty percent of the total information within an hour of intake. After twenty-one days, a huge percentage of the information has been lost, sometimes as high as eighty percent.

This is not to say that lectures have no place in training. There are a number of keys to making lectures more effective.

First, give homework prior to the lecture. This homework should introduce some basic principles that the trainee will learn. Definitions of terms, specific concepts with expla-

IN ESSENCE, LECTURING IS A DATA DUMP. THERE IS SO MUCH DATA WITHIN THESE LECTURES THAT A PERSON RARELY CAN RECALL EVEN SIXTY PERCENT OF THE TOTAL INFORMATION WITHIN AN HOUR OF INTAKE.

nations, and work flow charts provide context for the upcoming materials that will be represented in the lecture format. These items (and you may think of more that work in your specific instance) will allow participants to arrange data in a more organized fashion and relate it to a previous learning experience.

Second, shorten lectures to no more than an hour. This will lengthen the training process, but if the purpose of training is for employees to understand and retain the information, the benefits far outweigh the additional time. Participants can receive and grasp far more when the information is presented in small doses.

Third, restrict each lecture to no more than ten discussion points. Each major point can include additional subpoints. Participants can organize data in groupings of ten in an hour; beyond that, the level of learning declines at a significant and constant rate. Fewer than ten discussion points is preferred.

Fourth, create feedback mechanisms. This should happen on two levels: discuss how the points can actually be applied, and ensure that participants understand what they have learned. The application of information makes the training session valuable, so create a conversation about how employees will use the information on the job. Adults want to know why they need the information. The other feedback mechanism is to ask employees, "Do you understand?" You can take an indirect approach by inquiring if the participants have questions, but often participants don't want to betray that they are lost. Great trainers watch for confusion on the faces of their students. The trainer should always review to make certain that no one is confused. Don't worry about losing time by going back to explain. Review takes less time than correcting a problem on the job that results from not understanding the material.

Fifth, give examples. In fact, give a lot of examples. Examples provide context while also exposing trainees to the real-world situations they may face on the job. True examples that involve your company and its people work the best. Trainees need to know that what you preach is what happens at work.

Our HR trainees are told to make heroes of those who already work within the organization. Use names, dates, places, and actions to make the example come to life. It is always a delight to watch trainees enter the workplace and meet the people who were used as positive examples.

COACHING

Coaching is the most effective form of training because it offers comprehension and retention rates many times higher than lecture. This advantage hugely impacts what happens in the workplace. Effective coaching involves four steps: explanation, demonstration, application, and repetition.

Explanation is simply describing the "what" and the "why" of the concept being taught. Please do not forget the why (we have returned to "motive") because trainees tend to learn at a higher level of retention when they associate a "why" with a "what."

COACHING IS THE MOST EFFECTIVE FORM OF TRAINING BECAUSE IT OFFERS COMPREHENSION AND RETENTION RATES MANY TIMES HIGHER THAN LECTURE.

Whatever is being taught should be taught in detail. Repeat the description twice, using different words the second time.

Demonstration involves watching the instructor perform the task. Again, perform the task twice. Although we've already discussed the "why," explain again why we do it this way. This may involve regulations, policy, or the need for wide distribution of data, time-motion studies, and any number of other things.

Application involves the trainees performing the task with feedback from the instructor and other students. The involvement of other students is an effective additional teaching technique because the act of watching others for the purpose of providing critique forces the observing student to *think*. Imagine the novelty of asking a trainee to *think* during a training session!

Application is also an effective way to implant concepts and behaviors of the trainees. They remember what they saw and what they thought when they are looking for the positive and negative aspects of someone else's performance.

Repetition deals with application. As with almost anything we do in life, practice improves performance. For many tasks, particularly frontline tasks, enough repetition can make the task secondary and natural once the frontline employee hits the job site.

My personal experience is that coaching sessions work better if you have assigned two-person teams. This concept is stolen outright from the U.S. Navy SEALs training program. The SEALs assign "swim buddies" for the purpose of accountability. Each person is responsible for not only his own actions but also the actions of his buddy. Swim buddies work in corporate training as well. In fact, the quality of the training improves as each buddy pushes the other, supports the other, and affirms the other. Swim buddies may go out for lunch, drinks, or dinner, and a remarkable thing happens—they continue to discuss the training, further enforcing the information long after the training sessions have concluded.

So this works well, you think, for the minions at the bottom of the food chain. How can it work when training is aimed at people higher up? Fair enough. In reality, the same system works at all levels of management. There is no difference in the outcome, whether you are training a minimum-wage employee or a senior manager. The big difference is that the higher up you go in the organization, the less knowledge training and task training you need.

At the executive level, we should be constantly teaching communication principles and relationship-building skills. Lack of knowing how and when to communicate has dug a massive pothole in the executive highway, and people are having accidents. However, communication is not presently a core element of executive training, even though the vast majority of executives and employees cite good communication ability as a requisite for leading people. Relationship-building skills are also absent from most executive training modules because the skills are sometimes considered beneath the tough, rugged, command-modeled executive, which places executives and trainers in a deep zone of denial as to the realities of what drives human productivity.

Communication is a prime example of executive training that should use the elements of coaching. Learning the decision-making process, evaluating and improving corporate and departmental cultures, team building, project management, and other executive skills are best taught in a lecture/coaching/mentoring format. The difference between coaching and mentoring is the number of trainees involved and the time commitment. Coaching normally occurs over a short period of time with a group of people. Mentoring occurs over a long period of time and involves one-to-one tutoring.

LACK OF KNOWING HOW AND WHEN TO COMMUNICATE HAS DUG A MASSIVE POTHOLE IN THE EXECUTIVE HIGHWAY, AND PEOPLE ARE HAVING ACCIDENTS.

★ ★

IMPLEMENTATION: *Identify the employees with the greatest potential and coach to keep them.*

We all want to keep our good employees, which is one of a myriad of reasons given here for creating communication techniques that foster loyalty.

Although we have placed emphasis on the requirement to coach *them* to success, we should also emphasize the need to allow them to coach *us* to success. People in leadership positions are sometimes prone to lead with the mouth, but great leaders know to be humble enough to hear the ideas and concerns of employees. This is so rarely done that employees are often shocked when a CEO or department head walks in and asks, "So, what are your ideas or concerns?"

This was forcefully revealed to me when I took a management contract to operate a division until a permanent replacement could be located. Every employee under my leadership met with me in a small auditorium. I made three points:

1. *I am not here to bring about great change, only to hold the reins until a new leader is hired.* (This reduced fears of rumored layoffs.)
2. *I will assume everyone here is a professional until you prove me wrong. I will treat you with respect, courtesy, and even deference.* (This removed fears that remarks from upper tier management may influence how I perceived people.)
3. *This is the most talking I will do. From this point on, I am here to listen.* (People lowered their eyes or gave knowing looks to each other. No one believed I cared about their opinions.)

For two weeks I walked the halls asking for input and received none. Finally, after almost three weeks, four women came to me with a suggestion. I liked it and acted upon it at first opportunity. Before they left the office I inquired as to why it had taken so long to offer this wonderful idea. It was then that the obvious was confessed: they did not believe I would listen. It took two weeks of persistent pleas before they decided to give it a shot. After this meeting, walking around the division asking for suggestions was an exhilarating experience as people became eager for dialogue. Some good suggestions were too substantial for me to act on in my role as temporary executive director, but I took pains to explain that these ideas would have a long-term impact on the organization and would therefore violate my first promise to not bring about significant change. I promised to build a folder of these ideas and offer them to the permanent replacement.

★ ★

*The ability to perform tasks well does not qualify
an employee to assume a leadership position.*

ALTHOUGH THE CALL TO LEADERS TO ADOPT LEADERSHIP AS YOUR VOCATION
EXTENDS TO EVERYONE, there is a line of differentiation that should be drawn.
Leadership seized when opportunity arises is not to be confused with the requirements of leadership on a day to day basis. In all industries there is a tendency to
reward superior-tasking people with management positions once the dues have
been paid. This is a noble and just cause—on the surface.

When hiring for a management position that is also a leadership position,
usually meaning that the person is now responsible for managing and motivating staff, do not fall into the trap of believing that because the person can move
paper or fashion reports as an underling, the person is qualified to manage and
lead. Professional skill sets of a mechanical position are quite different from
managing and leading skills.

Many a poor promotion decision has been made because the different skills
required were not considered. The mistake is usually evident within a few months.
The problem is that upper management, having made the decision, faces the difficult task of what to do with this employee.

A recent seminar attendee related the story of her new vice president, a
well-liked man who was courteous, considerate, and a friend to all. The problem,
said the attendee, was that he so desperately wanted to be liked that he could
not make a decision for fear of
offending someone. This was
apparent from the first week
when directives were needed
from the VP so that a newly
formed task force could begin its work. Six weeks later the task force was still
inactive, as were several departments below the VP. Senior management knew
the hire was a bad one, but they waited for him to, in the words of the CEO to
some critics, "get up to speed." Months passed and the situation worsened. An
outside "executive coach" was hired to help the VP develop as a leader, but to no
avail. Eighteen months later, the VP was still around despite a dismal leadership
record. "The problem isn't him anymore," said the attendee. "The problem is that
the wimps above him don't have the courage to do the obvious. And those of us
who feel the pain every day are ready to jump this ship."

The idea may seem blasphemous, but here it is: *no one earns a promotion by
paying dues*. The example above demonstrates the person must be qualified to ful-

**THE IDEA MAY SEEM BLASPHEMOUS,
BUT HERE IT IS:** *NO ONE EARNS A PRO-
MOTION BY PAYING DUES.*

fill the responsibilities of the job. The move from the lower and middle levels of an organization to upper levels often requires a change in worldview. This shift in context from localized view to global view often makes for a difficult transition with the unfortunate result being that the longer the transition takes, the more disruption the organization experiences.

An organization faced this problem when it elevated a project director to director of a division involved in fifty projects. This individual had been stellar in handling a series of small, closed-end projects and a staff of seven people.

Suddenly, he was thrown into a job that required he lead multiple large, international projects and a staff many times larger than before.

The hands-on (read "little delegation of authority") techniques that made him successful at one level failed him in this larger setting. Nonetheless, he refused to let go of his previously successful management style. The resulting work schedule of fourteen-hour days, six days a week, left him exhausted, disorganized, and mentally incapable of making quick decisions.

Delegation was a concept absolutely foreign to his work experience, resulting in some projects falling behind schedule, many significantly behind schedule, because the people in the field waited for decisions to be made in an office two thousand miles away. Due to the hectic schedule he created for himself, he often had to cancel meetings, which destroyed the staff's time-sensitive deadlines, leaving people paralyzed in the office and in the field.

His one-dimensional communication style based upon command and control failed to adapt to different external project cultures, creating a series of misunderstandings that resulted in poor execution in the field and lost resources. Since this organization lacked leadership and communication training, the poor fellow was left to fend for himself. Overwhelmed by work and stress, he could not disengage long enough to learn from his experiences, so he repeatedly made the same mistakes that sent productivity into a downward spiral.

The fault here lies not with the employee but with the organization and its upper management for failing to consider the level of skill sets required to lead a large group involved in a global endeavor. Management never attempted to coach the executive before his ascent to the position, and failed to offer (and insist he engage in) training that would address his leadership deficiencies. In essence, they sent their version of Jeremiah Johnson into the wilderness, ill prepared to survive.

This scenario exists in almost every organization at some time or another. Before promoting anyone from task-centered employment to a leadership position, you must prepare for the promotion in two ways.

★ ★

IMPLEMENTATION:
*Prior to offering a promotion, place the employee
in charge of a project that requires people skills.*

Projects that can be successful without delegation and within the boundaries of command-and-control communication do not test the ability of this person to be successful in a broader venue, so be careful to watch carefully as the project is launched.

This test will signal the employee's readiness to ascend to a people-centered position. Then, once the promotion is offered but prior to the actual move, send the employee to a leadership training course that emphasizes communication skills and employee motivation techniques as well as project management skills.

Also, suggest a menu of books and articles that emphasize these same elements. It is the company's responsibility to prepare the newly promoted employee to succeed. On-the-job training may damage the reputation of the employee and the productivity of the organization, as has been previously explained, so it's important that no mistakes be made.

B UILDING THE RIGHT TEAM IS A NECESSARY PROCESS THAT ALL LEADERS MUST UNDERTAKE. When implemented, the concepts in this chapter will provide you with the following: the people necessary to implement your vision; improved performance of these people through ongoing training, including effective leadership training; an organization that stays energized and enthusiastic; and the right people in leadership positions, instead of those who are not ready.

CHAPTER SIX

★ ★ ★

COMMUNICATING
TO THE CULTURE

White Hat Principles:

★ *High-context communication is superior to low-context communication.*
★ *Truth and harmony cannot coexist.*
★ *Beware of stupid rules.*
★ *Keep what you tolerate.*
★ *Few corporate habits waste more time than meetings.*

MUCH OF WHAT HAS PRECEDED THIS CHAPTER RELATES TO COMMU-
NICATING WITHIN A CULTURE. The steps to promoting vision, clear
articulation of personal and corporate values, permission giving, and
leading with transparency all directly relate to clear and effective communication. The principles in this chapter delve deeper into these concepts, providing
new insights that will be valuable to your success as a White Hat leader.

The first principle recognizes that the quality of communication can be mea-
sured in degrees; the higher our understanding of the context through which
our employees filter information, the higher the quality of the communication
we provide. The second principle acknowledges that many cultures drive truth
underground in order to provide a superficial appearance of harmony. The third
principle recognizes that we invite dissent and employee "shortcuts" when we

substitute arrogance for credibility. The fourth principle reintroduces the need for courage to reject undesirable aspects of culture, while the fifth principle attacks the idea that more meetings result in better communication.

High-context communication is superior to low-context communication.

THE DIFFERENCE BETWEEN HIGH-CONTEXT AND LOW-CONTEXT COMMUNICA-TION IS MADE FORCEFULLY CLEAR IN THE FOLLOWING CASE. A federal agency realized it must reorganize in order to achieve the operational efficiencies that would satisfy Congressional funding sources. The agency message to Congress was to the point: reorganization of the department will occur over an eighteen-month period so that the agency will be more effective in delivering services to its "customers."

On the surface, the message appeared perfect. It contained the act (reorganization), the time frame (eighteen months), and the benefit of the action (effective delivery of services).

EMPLOYEES DON'T KNOW WHAT THEY DON'T KNOW, SO THE IMPACT OF CHANGE UPON THEM IS LEFT TO THEIR IMAGINATIONS, A SITUATION THAT GEN-ERATES A HIGH LEVEL OF PARANOIA IN LOW-CONTEXT ORGANIZATIONS.

Congress liked the message, as did the senior managers who drafted it.

Employees of the department absolutely panicked when they read the statement in the following morning's newspaper because their context was completely different from that of management and Congress: Will I lose my job? Even if I do not lose my job, will I be moved to another area or have to work under a new supervisor? Will my salary be affected?

The leadership failed to understand that a message suitable to one target audience might devastate another audience. Morale plummeted while turnover rates increased. Productivity declined as absenteeism escalated.

In truth, senior managers were looking at reorganization strategies that avoided lay-offs. It simply never dawned on the managers who knew the process and content of the decision making that employees needed to receive a message that contained additional information critical to that group.

Employees who work within low-context organizations become sensitive to and extremely concerned about any changes that take place within their department or within the broader organization. This is precisely because they receive so little information within their context. Employees don't know what they don't know, so the impact of change upon them is left to their imaginations, a situation that generates a high level of paranoia in low-context organizations. That change prompts people to leave the organization or, whenever possible, to slow the rate of change.

★ ★

IMPLEMENTATION: *Communicate with high context to lower the risk of dangerous miscommunication.*

The concepts of high and low context come from the work of anthropologists who deal with wider cultures than business organizations. Nonetheless, they apply to business and life.

The intent is to connect context with meaning. Placing messages in the context of the person or groups receiving the messages increases the chance of both parties, sharing the understanding of the message's meaning. When we don't achieve shared meaning, we have failed to achieve effective communication and will likely fail to achieve intended results.

High context means that the message is not restricted to the specifics of the words (words can also create a form of code). The connection goes beyond the words so the message is internalized, or has meaning in a direct fashion to that person's situation, experiences, or environment. The reorganization message examined above proved to be a high-context message to a Congress that was forcefully calling for a more lean and mean federal infrastructure. Conversely, it was a low-context message for employees.

Low context means that the words stand alone and naked, somewhat exposed to filter systems, and certainly to interpretation. The receiver of the message will, therefore, redefine its meaning to his or her situation, experiences, or environment.

In all cultures, high-context communication results in a more high-speed, low-drag, and satisfying workplace. High speed means that the organization moves with urgency because high-context communication allows everyone to act with certainty. Clear directions allow employees to operate without fear of being chastised for doing the wrong thing. Low-context communication creates drag within an organization. It slows progress, as employees must stop to ask permission for each new activity. An employee who is not sure about what he is doing and why will always move more cautiously out of fear. In some cases, low-context communication can cause temporary paralysis.

Anyone at any level can contribute to a high-context culture, but it is most likely to implant itself on a culture when top management exhibits it. Everyone underneath the executive suite takes cues from this approach, resulting in high-context communication being implanted in all levels of the organization. Not only do middle managers pick up on the process and begin to use it, the employees on the front lines eventually begin to use high context in their relations with customers.

The use of high-context communication improves the entire culture of relationships at all levels, with the significant side benefit of unifying staff as one cohesive force working together toward the organization's goals.

High context has the added benefit of effectively blunting what is commonly referred to as information overload. The problem of information overload is not, as is commonly believed, too much information. The overload occurs when we do not know what to do with all the information.

High-context organizations resolve the problem by revealing which information is important to know and not to know. It is the context of the information that matters.

★ ★

Truth and harmony cannot coexist.

HIGH-CONTEXT COMMUNICATION IS IMPOSSIBLE TO ACHIEVE when employees do not feel free to engage in open discussions that reveal disagreement.

Most of us want to work in a harmonious setting. We seek calm and we wish to like and to be liked by those with whom we associate at work.

Leaders too often fall into the trap of believing that harmony is a desired goal, one that affirms their ability to lead people. But often, harmony as a goal creates only surface calm while fostering a subterranean culture that lashes out its discontent in hallways and offices because these are the only places where disagreement can be safely aired. In fact, absolute harmony often creates a business model that sentences everyone to fall well short of their capabilities, and therefore results in the company or business unit falling well short of its potential productivity.

Dealing with the realities of business and life requires an environment of honesty created by leaders who are not afraid to expose and deal with the conflicts inherent in any organization populated by human beings.

It is easy to identify companies that care more about harmony than getting to the truth. The meetings are kiss-up, butt-covering events that avoid addressing the large elephants in the room.

It stimulates suck-up behavior. It tells employees, check your brain at the door and pucker your lips because you will be kissing someone's behind. Lost in this **HARMONY AS A GOAL CREATES ONLY SURFACE CALM WHILE FOSTERING A SUBTERRANEAN CULTURE THAT LASHES OUT ITS DISCONTENT.**

"harmony" is all the good that can come from direct conversation. Of course, direct conversation can lead to conflict and conflict makes people uncomfortable.

One company executive tells the story of working on a committee chaired by the VP of his division. The committee meetings were long, with random conversations resulting in little forward movement toward the goal. Each meeting ended with committee members reviewing their respective calendars to allow for yet another meeting.

The members were frustrated and restless as a result of unfocused leadership from the chair. Little work was assigned between meetings that might carry forward the agenda. Everyone in the room knew that the chair needed to be more focused and organized, and that some effort had to be made inside the meetings to avoid time-wasting tangents.

Despite the obvious, no committee member wanted to state the obvious— not because the chair was the boss, but because no one wanted to cause, in the executive's own words, "a problem."

"Our VP likes to joke and be one of the guys," he says. "He's uncomfortable when anyone seems the least unhappy. It's not just in this setting. It's true all the time. His mantra is 'Don't worry, be happy.' Any uncomfortable discussion draws a reprimand. That makes it impossible for the rest of us to point out a problem, much less to try to correct it."

The VP has created a culture that chooses harmony over truth. The result is wasted time and a frustrated staff. Far from creating harmony, the VP creates a negative culture inhabited by angry employees.

People tend to confuse harmony with a healthy respect and openness of communication. Transparency, a respectful ambience, and commitment to core values of the organization create a better definition for what harmony should be. Instead, the pursuit of harmony is often nothing more than being adept at dancing around and leaping over stinking elephants that are alive and well within an organization.

★ ★

IMPLEMENTATION: *Allow conflict.*

The amount of creativity and problem solving lost in the harmonious atmosphere of an organization is overwhelming. Perhaps we can make the transition by recognizing that conflict is the first step toward collaboration. We must know how each of us views an issue before we find where we agree, which in turn provides a platform for working together toward common goals.

True conflict is easily avoided by staying fixed on the issue while avoiding personal statements. "That's a stupid idea" is a statement that probably destroys future opportunity for dialogue. "Let's talk about that and see where it leads" opens doors to discourse.

★ ★

IMPLEMENTATION: *Truth + Variety = Creativity*

A culture based on harmony over truth also tends to develop the monotony necessary to keep all things in balance. This assembly-line approach may manifest itself in ways as simple as having staff meetings on the same day of week at the same time of day in the same room each time. Studies have shown that cultures of monotony inhibit creativity because it is the variety of life and business that inspires vitality and creativity. Remember this formula: Truth + Variety = Creativity.

★ ★

Beware of stupid rules.

PEOPLE TEND TO QUESTION THE LIMITS OF BOUNDARIES THAT HAVE BEEN SET. This is true across all generations, but is dominant within the newer generation of employees, as every employer and parent knows.

During a recent visit to a restaurant in Seattle, I became inadvertently privy to a conversation between a father and son, the "child" appearing to be about twenty years old. The father launched the first cannon shot with the observation that "elbows on the table are considered bad manners." The son had an immediate and generational response.

"Who made up that rule?" was his rebuttal. "That's a stupid rule! Why is it bad to have elbows on the table? Because someone said it's wrong, that's why, and the world just accepted it. Somebody should have said, 'Hey, that's a stupid rule,' then we wouldn't be having this stupid conversation."

The father calmly talked about the wisdom of establishing social norms and how norms and laws are the real foundations of civilization to which the son said, "We're talking about elbows here, okay? Civilization is not going to fall because of elbows."

At this moment, the young man drilled home an intelligent observation about culture.

"It's like the time I was in training at the bank and the trainer kept saying, 'Do this and do that,' and we'd ask, 'Why do it that way? Wouldn't it be easier to do it another way?' She said, 'We do it this way so you do it this way!'" He paused as he took a sip of water and caught his breath, before giving his eye-popping

PEOPLE TEND TO QUESTION THE LIMITS OF BOUNDARIES THAT HAVE BEEN SET. THIS IS TRUE ACROSS ALL GENERATIONS, BUT IS DOMINANT WITHIN THE NEWER GENERATION OF EMPLOYEES, AS EVERY EMPLOYER AND PARENT KNOWS.

conclusion. "If you don't know why you have a rule then it is a stupid rule," the young man stated in a matter-of-fact voice. "We all talked about it after class and we all agreed that it's okay to look for a better way if they can't even tell us why we have to do it their way."

This conversation drew out a distant memory of a training session I had observed several years before, during which trainees asked about why a certain procedure was being taught when it appeared that other options might be better. The trainer had responded, "This is the way we do it." It was obvious from the looks on their faces that the trainees found this answer unsatisfying.

Still later, there appeared to be a theme emerging among clients that "this generation does not listen to us, choosing to do things the way they want to do them instead how we think they should be done." If this observation is true, there is a culture issue that should be examined, defined, and addressed.

The young man at lunch offered a revelation when he said, "If you don't know why you have a rule, then it is a stupid rule." In addition, the stupidity of the rule is viewed as implied permission to "look for a better way."

Let's summarize the findings in this scenario. First, the organization has rules it cannot justify (or, the people who state the rules to others do not know the justification behind those rules). Second, the new generation of employees, a subset of the organization's culture, rejects the rules that have no justification. Third, the new generation views absence of justification as permission to ignore the rules (sometimes a process) and instead seek a better alternative. Fourth, management views this pursuit of the better way as proof that "they do not listen to us."

From these observations, it follows that the organization has lost credibility with the new generation because the organization is making up rules and processes without reason. That reaction is wholly understandable, and who is to say that it is wrong? After all, if the organization cannot articulate why it wants something performed a certain way maybe it is a stupid rule and perhaps other approaches are superior! The fault for this condition is not with the younger employees but is with the organization that does not recognize this aspect of its culture and then respond to it.

Once the "why" question has entered the new-generation employee's brain, it is only a matter of time before the employee will try to shortcut or otherwise tinker with the process.

★ ★

IMPLEMENTATION: *Is there a reason for the rule?*

A trainer once observed during a training session, "I don't know why we do it that way and nobody else does either." This is a wonderful discovery! Now you are free to reinvent the process as you choose, as long as you have a reason for what you do.

If the reason for a rule or process is known, it should be shared with the employee(s). This additional information should automatically be a part of the conversation because it takes more time and money to solve problems created by an employee's "improvements" than it does to answer the "why" question from the beginning.

★ ★

Keep what you tolerate.

THE BEST COURSE TO A POSITIVE CULTURE INVOLVES (1) articulating the value system that defines acceptable attitudes and behaviors, (2) incorporating positive language into a culture, (3) reinforcing what is acceptable, and (4) rejecting what is not acceptable.

The first three steps are not easy, but the fourth step contains some serious issues for the leader who is not committed to a healthy culture for the organization. Rejecting the values, attitudes, behaviors, and language of other people requires a clear vision and strong dose of courage because it will likely result in anxiety and conflict. Yet, for a leader to be hero, he must rally people to a culture that they can embrace; a place that gives them purpose beyond the job and security beyond a paycheck. These things are not possible when others within the culture cause dissonance by operating outside the environment that is desired. These people are bacteria eating away at the foundation that will launch increased productivity and greater employee loyalty. If allowed to continue, the negative influences will overwhelm the positive until the workplace becomes an area filled with tension, personal agendas, and deceit.

The principle here is that you keep what you tolerate because allowing undesirable actions inside the culture gives permission for that behavior to be repeated and, ultimately, duplicated by others.

★ ★

IMPLEMENTATION: *Respond immediately to undesirable elements.*

Do this in a considerate way at first but more aggressively if repeated or duplicated. It takes just a slight nudge for most people to back away, although there are those who will push back. Place your value system out front as the definition of what is expected and continually refer back to it.

We've discussed putting the value system in writing and having employees sign an agreement to support the values. This is particularly effective inside cultures that are struggling with the impact of negative influences; it allows the leader to take the high moral ground in future discussions by beginning with the statement: "You committed to these values when you signed on the line. How much is your promise worth?"

★ ★

Few corporate habits waste more time than meetings.

I WAS TEMPTED TO TITLE THIS SECTION "More Communication Is Not Better Communication." Meetings come from the belief that the more we look at each other, the better we will perform. This is a fallacy of the highest order. Many of us have departed from meetings wondering why we spent one or two precious hours to accomplish nothing. The next time you are in such a meeting, calculate the amount of productivity and money that is lost by estimating an hourly rate for each person in the room and the amount of time spent by each person. Let's say we have six people in a meeting for two hours, each person having an average rate of fifty dollars per hour (not a high figure for executives). This meeting is costing the organization six hundred dollars and twenty-four hours of productivity. Now multiply that by the number of unproductive meetings the group has had in a month or a year. Meetings are an investment of time and resources, so they should be held only when they will provide a return on investment.

MEETINGS COME FROM THE BELIEF THAT THE MORE WE LOOK AT EACH OTHER, THE BETTER WE WILL PERFORM. THIS IS A FALLACY OF THE HIGHEST ORDER.

A recent meeting I had with a client to decide the next steps on a project became a showcase for waste when the client invited six staff members to join us. None of the six said a word during the meeting because none had a viable reason for attending. Afterwards, two stopped me in the hall to ask about their attendance. Had they missed something? All I could do was thank them for their time, which undoubtedly could have been better used elsewhere.

To prevent wasted time and money, ask yourself this basic question: "Do we need a meeting for this particular issue?" Most meetings are about sharing information that can be distributed more efficiently in e-mail or office mail.

Imagine the hours you have spent in meetings receiving documents that someone else reads or summarizes for you. You can read, so what sense does it make to have a meeting? It makes more sense to have a meeting to discuss the impact of the information you have read, although that discussion, too, may be more efficiently handled by other means.

The best meetings are those that involve decisions, either those made or those being made during the course of the meeting. Today, most meetings are largely an arcane habit left over from days prior to technology. Keep in mind that technology has changed the way we communicate.

★ ★

IMPLEMENTATION: *Make sure meetings are effective.*

When you have determined the need for a meeting, consider these six elements to having an effective meeting.

1. *There are expectations for a specific outcome(s).* If there are no outcomes, there should not be a meeting.
2. *Start on time.* Do not ignore latecomers—feel free to admonish those who do not respect the time of others. Do not review the discussion points they have missed; instead, tell them to stay late so you can tell them. They will not be late next time.
3. *Don't try to do too much.* The more you try to accomplish, the less you will accomplish. Stay focused on the outcomes.
4. *Establish a quitting time.* This creates a sense of urgency that results in more focus among the participants.
5. *Always summarize the assignments or actions that should come next.* Be specific by stating who, what, and when.
6. *Circulate to all participants a summary of the meeting.*

In addition, ask yourself these core questions:

Before the meeting
1. *What is the anticipated outcome?*
2. *Who needs to be present?*
3. *How will they be motivated to participate?*

During the meeting
1. Is everyone's viewpoint in the open?
2. Is everyone participating?

After the meeting
1. What is the level of buy-in?
2. Is there a sense of urgency?

Meetings with purpose that promote discussion and reach an out-come are meetings worth having. These questions, when applied, will prevent those meetings that end with people thinking they wasted their time. Anytime you call an unnecessary meeting, you are losing productivity. Anytime you call a meeting that enhances productivity, you are a hero.

★ ★

G REAT COMMUNICATION IS THE RESULT OF CLEARLY ARTICULATED MESSAGES that are presented in the highest context and are delivered consistently over a long period of time. Implementation of concepts such as the feedback loop, open motive (these concepts are discussed in Chapter 7), and high-context communication are easy to do once we embrace these concepts and make persistent efforts to incorporate them. These pragmatic tools of leadership can begin positively impacting your own leadership abilities the first moment you use them. The challenge is to lead yourself to use the tools.

CHAPTER SEVEN

★ ★ ★

COMMUNICATING
WITH INDIVIDUALS

White Hat Principles:

★ *Rethink the communication model.*
★ *Give specific instructions.*
★ *Use open motive.*
★ *Respond to high-touch needs.*

IN THIS CHAPTER, we shift the focus away from broader cultural issues and toward communicating with individuals. The first principle refutes the traditional model that defines effective communication by adding a step that will make your life easier. The second principle reveals that most of us think we give specific instructions but actually are ambiguous with our language. The third principle offers the step most often missing in directing employees. The fourth principle recognizes that great leaders must give time to those who need it most.

Rethink the communication model.

ANYONE WHO HAS TAKEN A BASIC COMMUNICATION CLASS KNOWS THE BASIC COMMUNICATION MODEL WHICH CONSISTS OF SENDER----MESSAGE----RECEIVER.

The model proposes that communication takes place when Person A sends a message to Person B. Anyone who has been married for more than five minutes knows this is not true!

My job demands that I travel upwards of two hundred days a year. When I have time at home I tend to sit in my wingback leather recliner in front of the television set, watching a sports event. The event is irrelevant because this is about creating "my time" to relax and go brain-dead. The world of business is tuned out as I create a private world of isolation.

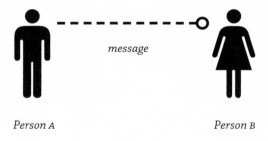

message

Person A   *Person B*

Sometimes during these periods of internal nothingness, my wife chooses to engage in conversation. The problem is *not* that I am unaware of her—she is obviously talking. It is just that she is background noise, simple static buzzing around my head as would a gnat. All I hear is "blah blah blah."

Most husbands and wives experience these moments of noncommunicative conversation. The only words that the husband ever clearly understands are these: "What do you think?"

Now I'm in trouble. I'm in danger of being fully exposed as a nonparticipant in what has been a two- to three-minute one-sided attempt at marital dialogue. I have two choices. I can confess to this slight by asking, "Were you talking to me?" which places me in an untenable position as a lout and an insufferably selfish husband, or I can escape by saying, "That sounds good to me." I did that a few years ago and the next thing I knew I had a puppy.

These one-sided "conversations" happen every day at home and at work. The communication model supposes that communication has taken place as Person A (spouse, employee, leader) delivers a message (a directive, a question, neutral information) to Person B (spouse, employee, leader). Obviously, despite the accepted model, no communication has occurred!

The core element missing from the communication model is the *feedback loop*. The feedback loop ends each conversation with a review of what we *think* was said. It is amazing how many times the simple insertion of feedback reveals how poorly we communicated.

A CEO sat across his desk from an employee and explained the formation of a new project. The CEO believed he was clearly revealing the details. He concluded by saying, "We need to get off to a quick start by having a draft of the implementation strategy for review by Monday." The employee responded, "Yes, I agree."

The following Monday when the CEO walked into the same employee's office to request the draft, he was met with a surprising response.

"I didn't realize you wanted *me* to write the draft," said the employee. "I thought you were keeping me in the loop."

In any business, people spend and waste a great deal of time on following up with those who listened to the conversation but did not hear the message. Deadlines are missed. Assignments are not correctly fulfilled, and the result is yet another meeting, more follow-up e-mails, phone calls, hallway conversations—all necessary because there was no feedback loop. Every minute of time used in these endeavors is a minute of productivity lost.

★ ★

IMPLEMENTATION: *Use the feedback loop.*

The feedback loop resolves the issue of so many items "falling through the cracks." The implementation of the loop is amazingly simple—at the end of the discussion ask, "What did you hear?" You will be jolted by the number of times the response is not what you expect. You will also have an opportunity to correct misunderstandings then and there, thereby significantly decreasing the risk of anything falling through the cracks. It also results in fewer follow-up meetings, the necessity of going back and doing things over, and the frustration of using valuable time to go over the same thing a second or third time.

Some seminar participants have sometimes objected to the feedback loop, saying that they don't have time to perform this simple task. The reality is that people who are task saturated are the very people who should be using the loop. Take two minutes at the end of a conversation to create feedback, and you will save hours of follow-up every month, thereby increasing your productivity as well as the productivity of your employees.

As with most communication models, this works both ways, so when your boss gives you direction, insert your own feedback loop by saying, "Let me review this assignment to make sure I have it," then deliver a summary. Again, you will prevent wasted time from misunderstandings.

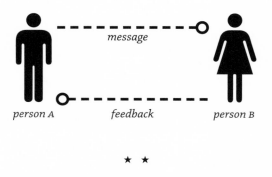

person A   feedback   person B

★ ★

Give specific instructions.

MANAGERS AND LEADERS OFTEN USE DIRECTIVE LANGUAGE TOWARD EMPLOYEES, meaning that they tend to, in simple terms, give an order. The order, which almost always asks for a desired outcome, appears specific to the manager but is ambiguous to the employee.

A classic example occurred when a bank executive called his chief loan officer into the office for a conversation. "We've got to ramp up a bit, Paul," said the executive. "I have to give a report to the board and that group is going to want better numbers than we have. Here's the bottom line: get more loans."

At first review, this may seem to be a high-context message, as (1) the subject of loans is immediately relevant to a loan officer, (2) the point of concern (the board wants better numbers) is provided, and (3) the assignment (get more loans) seems specific. In reality, it is a low-context message because it does not consider the situation of the loan officer.

Paul, the loan officer, walked out of the conversation with more questions than answers: What kind of loans are of interest to the board? Without that answer Paul is left to only guess where his effort should be applied. How many loans will satisfy the board?

Without a target number Paul has no definition for success. What is the deadline for achieving this success? Paul is not given the date of the board meeting so he has no idea how

YOU, AS A LEADER, MUST TAKE THE RESPONSIBILITY TO STEP BACK AND ASSESS HOW YOUR EMPLOYEES WILL FILTER YOUR INSTRUCTIONS FROM THEIR POSITIONS WITHIN THE ORGANIZATION.

much planning and implementation time he has been given. How does Paul increase the number of loans without a change in the way he is doing business? Paul is already working at full speed, so he needs to know the resources he is being offered that will increase his chance for success.

The loan officer did what he could with what he had, but he did not satisfy the executive because the executive did not provide specific directions. Without this benefit, the loan officer succeeded in getting more loans, technically satisfying the directive from his boss, but they were not the kinds of loans or of the volume desired by the boss. Although Paul was criticized for this failure, the fault lies not with the loan officer but with the executive who used low-context communication that created not only a sense of ambiguity but also a sense of frustration from Paul, who did what he was told but still failed in the eyes of his supervisor.

★ ★

IMPLEMENTATION: *Consider the employee's context to ensure clarity of directions.*

As often happens in business, the bank executive believed he was offering a specific message while instead creating ambiguity. His failure, however, could have been overcome by Paul applying the feedback loop, a two-minute conversation that would answer his questions and thereby remove all ambiguity from the instruction.

Precise and consistent messaging defeats highly developed filter systems. In order to be precise, the leadership team must understand and communicate within the context in which others are likely to hear the messages.

This leads to the observation that in addition to using the feedback loop, the executive is obligated to understand Paul's context. The very fact that so many obvious questions remained unanswered reveals a nonleader in a leadership position. He seems to have no clue that his actions doom Paul to failure; indeed, he blamed Paul for the failure to satisfy the board. The lesson here is that you, as a leader, must take the responsibility to step back and assess how your employees will filter your instructions from their positions within the organization. It is impossible to consistently and effectively communicate in a high-context fashion until you complete this task.

The view and context at the top is quite different from that elsewhere in a company. The people at the top deal with different issues, pay attention to different things, and work in a broader context than the employees who follow them. This additional knowledge creates a higher context for the messages they receive. A different context results in a different interpretation of the same message. A message from the top of an organization often results in unintended consequences when it reaches employees who work in a limited area of responsibility.

Reorganization to those at the top means much-needed corporate efficiencies will be achieved. Employees at the bottom do not know the tactical strategy for that statement, so they view reorganization as shake-ups, new bosses, and lost jobs. Sharing the tactical response, which protected jobs, would have avoided the resulting internal turmoil.

The need for more loans at the top means a magic number by a deadline. To an underling it means confusion and frustration because there is no definition for success.

★ ★

Use open motive.

THE ABSENCE OF HIGH-CONTEXT COMMUNICATION CAN CREATE MANY PROBLEMS, even in a scenario that seems to involve the simplest and most obvious instructions. For example, a marketing directive from the top can be totally misunderstood at the bottom without consideration of how the message is filtered by frontline employees.

A financial institution finds itself in need of generating new deposits, so the executive suite decides that this can be accomplished by offering a highly desirable CD rate, one significantly higher than that presently offered. Remember, the *motive* of the higher rate is to attract new money to the institution. The key word here is "new."

The resulting directive from the top to the frontline people is simple and straightforward—sell a higher rate of CD. The frontline people dutifully go about the task. When preexisting CD customers walk through the door, they are met with an offer they cannot refuse.

"I see you have a low CD rate," says the customer service representative. "Wouldn't you rather have a higher CD rate?"

The customer gasps at this astounding offer and immediately accepts, after all there remains twelve months (or more) on the existing CD, so a move to a higher rate without penalty is a fabulous offer.

At the end of a thirty-day campaign to raise more cash, the financial institution has about the same amount of cash it had before the campaign, but now it is costing the institution more to have it. Instead of offering the higher rate to only new customers, the customer service representatives allowed existing customers to take advantage of it, defeating the motive for creating the higher rate CD.

The disconnection between upstairs leaders and downstairs followers occurred in the messaging. The executives simply told the customer reps to sell the new CD because it was obvious to them why this move was necessary. The customer reps, however, had a job to do, which was to sell. That was the context through which they heard their instructions, and without the introduction of a new context, that was the filter system through which the message flowed. Although the people in the executive suite were furious by the actions of the front line, the reality is that the customer reps did a superb job of pushing the CD to the customers, succeeding within the context of how they understood the assignment.

The lesson to embrace is that a highly specialized filter system obliterates organizational messages unless a new context is introduced.

★ ★

IMPLEMENTATION: *Establish open motive by answering the "why" question.*

The response to the CD example is to provide an open motive for the directive from the top. The instruction that stated "sell a higher rate CD" likely would have been successful with the addition of "so we can generate new deposits." With the addition of six words that answer the "why" question, the workers receiving the assignment would have known the CD is about new money rather than redirecting old money.

The idea of providing motive works on many levels. My friend Randy Harrington, CEO of Extreme Arts & Sciences, tells the story of being in his lawyer's office late one morning. The lawyer turned to his assistant, Debbie, and said, "Debbie, I want you to go to the basement and find the file on the Methodist Hospital case. Pull out the transcript of Jim Bloomer and get it to me." She said she would. Thirty minutes later the lawyer was searching for Debbie and the file. He had a prear-ranged phone call with another lawyer to discuss the transcript. Debbie, it was discovered, had gone to lunch. Her boss was furious.

When Debbie returned, she was greeted by a torrent of obscenities. After the scene had played for a minute or so, my friend Randy said, "Debbie, what if he had said, 'Go to the basement, find the Methodist Hospital file, and pull out the transcript of Jim Bloomer. I have a call in twenty minutes and I'll need that file.'"

"Oh," said Debbie, "I would have gotten it immediately."

She would have gotten it immediately because she would have known the motive behind the request. Debbie is a busy woman with many responsibilities and she, as with all other employees, has to prior-itize her activities according to what she knows. She made her decision about the file according to what she knew at the time of the request.

Who was at fault at the lawyer's office? Not Debbie. The lawyer learned a lesson about using motive as a way to help an employee be more efficient in her work and responsive to his needs, as well as one about clarity of communication and expectations.

Remember that people operate in the context they know. When they know motive (why), they know context, and therefore can per-form at the level you need.

Respond to high-touch needs.

THIS PRINCIPLE WAS ALMOST INCLUDED IN THE FIRST PART OF THIS CHAPTER because the need for constant feedback is ubiquitous among new-generation employees, hence the term "high touch." Observation verifies that older work-ers desire feedback as well, as most people want to know if their performance is acceptable to the chief decision makers.

A restaurant manager tells the story of interviewing a young applicant for the position of busboy. The interview went well; the young man was obviously bright and well-intentioned, reasonably well-dressed, and articulate. The manager reviewed a few key personnel rules before handing his happy new employee two sheets listing some dos and don'ts.

The young man walked to the car, tossing the two sheets into the backseat before cranking up his CD player and driving away. He had no intention of reading the list of dos and don'ts because he had listened closely to what the manager had to say and assumed that the manager told him everything that was important.

The first day on the job the youngster was approached by the manager. "Hey, you're not supposed to wear that kind of blue jeans to work," said the manager.

The employee was confused. "Sir? What's wrong with these?"

"Our rules say that jeans cannot be faded, must not have holes, and the hems must not go below the tops of your tennis shoes for sanitary reasons. Your jeans are faded, have holes in some exotic locations, and the hems are dragging on the floor. Why are you wearing those jeans?"

The youngster had what he considered an acceptable response. "You didn't tell me that I couldn't wear these jeans!"

"I didn't tell you verbally, but I gave you two sheets of rules. Look at number four on the list. Now, go home and change your jeans."

A few days later the manager again approached the employee. "What's with the apron? It's a mess!"

"Yes sir," came the response. "It kind of got dirty yesterday."

"We have a rule that you have to wash your apron after your shift. No one wants to see a dirty busboy walking around a restaurant."

The young employee was flustered and frustrated. "No one told me to wash my apron. No one told me!"

Again, the manager told the employee, "It's on the list. You need to read the list!"

The manager sums his experience this way: "These youngsters want you to tell them everything. It's high maintenance, but it is necessary because that age group is the only one who will take these jobs. I can yell, push, and beg, but they aren't going to change for me. I have to adapt to them. You give them a written set of rules and you know what they'll do with it? They'll toss it in the backseat of the car and that's where it will stay until they quit six months later. It's like the kid I was telling you about. He had a message that was 'nobody told me.' We have to hear that attitude and respond to it."

HIGH-TOUCH EMPLOYEES EXIST IN EVERY GENERATION, but it can be argued that the majority of employees would prefer more positive association with the boss, and this is what a great leader promotes. The drawback is that this approach takes time. However, as with most "extra steps" that improve culture, the extra effort saves effort in the long run, making the trade-off more than worthwhile. Recall that leadership is about relationships and high-touch methods will be affirmed.

★ ★ ★

TAKE ACTION

White Hat Principle:

★ *Good leaders take responsibility for making good things happen.*

I HOPE THAT AT THIS POINT, you have accepted that leadership is your vocation and have determined that you will operate with integrity and transparency in order to build positive relationships with employees. You now know that creating and implementing a strong system of values will give your employees direction and a common bond. You know that collaborating with employees on the vision means they will all feel that they can contribute and buy into that vision. You have also learned the importance of fostering an environment of high-context communication that includes open motive, recognizing the cravings each employee has from the job, and analyzing your office culture so you can make improvements. Now is the time for action.

Good leaders take responsibility for making good things happen.

"THE COWARDS NEVER STARTED AND THE WEAK DIED ALONG THE WAY," wrote author Stephen Crane, describing the journey westward in the days of wagon trains. Indeed, leadership as a vocation places great demands on those who wish to travel that road.

Maybe it is easier to let life unfold without our input. We can place the responsibility on "them," those other people, to do what they are supposed to do without our having to lead them. And perhaps, through some act of randomness, we will emerge as a leader in someone's eyes.

White Hat leaders know it isn't about "them." It's about us. They take responsibility for making good things happen. They apply the knowledge.

There is no single book or lecture or conference that gives all the answers to all the questions about leadership. Even if such a thing existed, it would be worthless without applying what you know.

Most of the people with whom you come into contact go through learning experiences with some degree of patience, but with no intention of making the effort to utilize their knowledge. The reason is simple: it's hard work. Leadership takes a degree of commitment not found in most, a commitment that takes courage to begin and persistence and patience to implement. Few can start the journey and fewer still can stay with it.

In the words of Oliver Wendell Holmes, "What lies behind us and what lies before us are tiny matters compared to what lies within us." Everyone has the ability to be a leader. It is simply a matter of becoming internally motivated to do it while possessing the attitude to do it well.

As a fellow traveler who understands the challenges inherent in this assignment, I leave you with this personal note. I never wanted to take the journey I have suggested to you. In fact, I fought the concept for many years. Through years of working with organizations, I became sensitive to lost potential, both on an individual and corporate level. The fear of ending my working life with regrets began to haunt me, so I took my own advice. It was one of the best decisions I've ever made.

A few months ago I was meeting with an executive of a national media firm. She leaned toward me from behind her massive desk and said, "Okay, leadership guru, what's the one thing that will make me a great leader?"

My response was as much for me as for her: "Don't settle for less than that."

★★★

Works Cited

INTRODUCTION: LEADING CULTURES

1. Edward T. Hall. *The Silent Language.* New York: Doubleday, 1959.
2. John P. Kotter. *Leading Change.* Boston: Harvard Business School Press, 1996.
———. *A Force for Change: How Leadership Differs from Management.* Free Press, 1990.
3. Marshall Goldsmith. "Becoming a Soft-Side Accountant." *Fast Company,* September 2003, 110.
4. Edward T. Hall. *The Silent Language.* New York: Doubleday, 1959.
5. Adrian Gostick and Chester Elton. *Managing with Carrots: Using Recognition to Attract and Retain the Best People.* Salt Lake City: Gibbs Smith, 2001.
6. Steven J. Stein and Howard E. Book. *The EQ Edge: Emotional Intelligence and Your Success.* Hoboken, New Jersey: Wiley, 2006.

CHAPTER 1: CHANGE THE WAY YOU THINK ABOUT LEADERSHIP

1. Clay Christensen. "The Industrialized Revolution." By Polly LaBarre. *Fast Company,* November 2003, 114.

2. Bob Nelson. "How to Lead Now." By John A. Byrne. *Fast Company,* August 2003, 62.

CHAPTER 2: PREPARE TO LEAD

1. James Champy. "The Hidden Qualities Of Great Leaders." *Fast Company,* November 2003, 135.

CHAPTER 3: TRAITS OF EFFECTIVE LEADERS

1. Peter Koestenbaum. "Do You Have the Will to Lead?" By Polly LaBarre. *Fast Company,* February 2000, 222.

2. Jeanie Daniel Duck. *The Change Monster: The Human Forces that Fuel or Foil Corporate Transformation and Change.* New York: Three Rivers Press, 2001.

3. Leonard Sweet. *AquaChurch: Essential Leadership Arts for Piloting Your Church in Today's Fluid Culture.* Loveland, CO: Group Publishing, 1999.

4. Adrian Gostick and Dana Telford. *The Integrity Advantage: How Taking the High Road Creates a Competitive Advantage in Business.* Salt Lake City: Gibbs Smith, 2003.

5. Ibid.

6. T. S. Eliot. "Shakespeare and the Stoicism of Seneca." *Selected Essays 1917–1932.* New York: Harcourt Brace & Company, 1934.

7. Jim Collins. *Good to Great: Why Some Companies Make the Leap...and Others Don't.* New York: HarperCollins, 2001.

8. Jerome Kohlberg. "Cheat Sheet." By Carleen Hawn. *Fast Company*, November 2003, 45.

CHAPTER 4: GIVE YOUR EMPLOYEES WHAT THEY NEED

1. Adrian Gostick and Chester Elton. *Managing with Carrots: Using Recognition to Attract and Retain the Best People.* Salt Lake City: Gibbs Smith, 2001.

2. John A. Byrne. "How to Lead Now." *Fast Company*, August 2003, 62.

3. Jon R. Katzenbach. *Why Pride Matters More Than Money: The Power of the World's Greatest Motivational Force.* New York: Crown Business, 2003.

4. John A. Byrne. "How to Lead Now." *Fast Company*, August 2003, 62.

CHAPTER 5: GATHERING THE TEAM

1. Chuck Pappalardo. "Test of Character." By Keith H. Hammonds. *Fast Company*, November 2003, 40.

Additional Resources

Collins, Jim and Jerry I. Porras. *Built to Last: Successful Habits of Visionary Companies*. New York: HarperCollins, 1994.

Dalai Lama. *Ethics for the New Millennium*. New York: Riverhead Books, 1999.

Martoia, Ron. *Morph: The Texture of Leadership for Tomorrow's Church*. Loveland, CO: Group Publishing, 2002.

Index